Getting to the Core: Reflections on Teaching and Learning

PRINTED IN THE UNITED STATES OF AMERICA

Visit our website at http://www.LearnerAssociates.net

First edition published 2005
by
LearnerAssociates.net
1962 Pawnee Trail
Okemos, Michigan 48864 USA

Getting to the Core: Reflections on Teaching and Learning

S. Joseph Levine

LearnerAssociates.net

PREFACE

For much of the 90s I was fortunate to have the opportunity to coordinate a monthly mailing designed specifically for new staff members of the Cooperative Extension Service in Michigan. The mailing consisted of an essay to assist the new staff in better understanding their role as educators and to challenge them to consider new and different ways of thinking about that role.

Rather naively I assumed that I could entice a variety of colleagues to take turns in writing the monthly essays. I would then be responsible for filling in as necessary. As it turned out I was only successful in a few cases (very few) and ended up writing most of the essays myself.

Within a few months I developed a set of guidelines that would help focus my efforts. First, the essays had to be fairly short – no one wanted to read lengthy prose. They had to be direct and to the point. Second, each essay needed to encourage a concern for reflection – the value of reflection in education and how to use reflection to inform our practice. Third, since most extension educators had a strong disciplinary background (agronomy, child development, animal science, etc.) the essays had to represent the human side, rather than the technical side, of what they were expected to do. The essays had to focus on helping people learn and change. And fourth, each essay should have a sense of lightness, a touch of humor, in an attempt to be disarming and therefore encourage the educator to "listen" to what was being said. After all, no one would voluntarily read a lecture.

Through the years the essays developed a following. I would receive emails from readers sharing their own experiences as an educator or encouraging me to focus on certain topics. Different readers would have their favorites – a particular essay that had special meaning for them. And periodically I would hear from someone who had misplaced a certain essay and hoped that I might be able to send them a replacement.

Finally, after much procrastinating, I've spent the necessary time to select, edit and update a good sized handful of the essays for sharing in this book. I've changed a few names, here and there, to protect the innocent. However, the original guidelines have been maintained.

It is my hope that these essays will strike a chord in you as they have so many times for me. The topics are diverse yet the focus continues as it always has – encouraging the reader to take a few minutes to reflect on their role as an educator.

I hope you will enjoy reading and reflecting on the essays as much as I enjoyed writing them.

S. Joseph Levine
February 2005

TABLE OF CONTENTS

1. The Problem Is You Write For The Moment And Not For The Generation

The challenge of developing educational programs with a vision for the future.

It came to me while I was listening to the local Public Radio station. It was an interview with a leading politician in the Middle East and his words sort of crept out before the interviewer knew what was happening! The interviewer was trying to push the politician into a corner and get him to react about a minor issue that was getting a lot of headlines. Before the interviewer knew what was happening the politician, using a quiet but strong voice, said:

"Why don't you look at the bigger picture once in a while? Journalists seem so focused on what is happening at this very instant that they seem to miss the larger view. You focus on the small details in an attempt to create large headlines without seeing the greater changes that are occurring all around you. It's as if the bigger picture isn't as startling a story and it's not worth reporting. You end up by writing for the moment and not for the hour, or the week, or the year or the generation. If we all focused on the moment, as you do, progress would be very haphazard. True, there would be lots of glamorous headlines, but there would be minimal long term change. And, we would leave very little for the next generation."

I was struck by the simplicity of his comments yet the realization that he could be addressing so many different groups with the same challenge. And, of course, as an educator the challenge was clear - we must learn not to educate for the moment but to educate for the generation.

1

When we educate for the moment we are concerned with focusing on small issues that have little long term consequence. They are the educational programs that we often call "busy work." They usually get us a lot of short term recognition. However, they usually eat up our time and when we're finished they leave little trace of their existence. Educating for the moment is education without a concern for vision. It is education that seems to provide immediate answers yet little potential for making the types of lasting change that we always hope for.

We must educate for the generation! We must be able to develop our ability to step away from what we're planning. And when we step away we have to look into the future. Our vision of the future must be that which guides us in the present. We must educate for the generation and not for the moment.

Sounds easy doesn't it? Just a bit of rearranging of goals, right? Well, the truth is there are a number of essential questions that we must be able to answer before we can truly begin to educate for the generation. Here are a few of them:

- Are we looking ahead to the potential long term effects of what we're doing? What do we see?
- Are others that we're working with able to see beyond the immediate and look to the long term effects? How can we help those around us to better see the long term potential of a project?
- Will it be possible to keep the educational program sustained long enough until the long term values begin to be seen? Are there things that we could be doing to help guarantee that a project's long term value is realized?
- Have we been able to create a balance between our short term projects (teaching for the moment) and our long term initiatives (teaching for the generation)? How can we improve the balance?

And finally,

- When we look ahead to the long term, do we like what we see? Is there anything we want to change now - while we still have a chance?

2. Transparent Programming

Too often the role of the educator gets in the way of learning!

The other day I reached for some Scotch tape and was disappointed to see that it was a roll of the old shiny type. (You know, the type that has a high gloss finish and darkens with age.) I had assumed that I had a roll of the newer type of tape - the kind that's just about invisible after you stick it on something. I really like the newer type because it works great and, unless you look really close, you don't even know that tape has been used! What a great product - the best tape is the kind that you can't see!

This stimulated my thinking and I started to try and identify other things that improved as they became more transparent. Window glass was an easy choice - it was so similar to tape. Then I thought of a television set and how a fuzzy picture was so annoying to watch. Or, how about a perfect fitting suit. If it was just right you hardly noticed it on your body - almost as if it were transparent.

Now I was on a roll! How about my favorite automatic teller machine. I can operate it wearing a blindfold. In a matter of a few seconds I can replenish my supply of pocket money and hardly notice that I even did it. It's as if the process was transparent. Driving my car, taking the exact same route to work each morning, heading to the same parking space - all processes that have become so familiar to me and comfortable that it's as if they have become transparent.

Then it struck me. As an educator we are often at our best if we are transparent for our learners. In other words, the best type of educational programming is that which is transparent and doesn't get in the way of the learners as they make use of the learning resources. Our role in the learning situation must be to empower the learner to access learning resources and to do it in the most expedient and transparent manner.

Too often we work to create a role for ourselves that becomes so significant that it actually can get in the way of the learner getting to the resources. We force people to sit quietly as we lecture on and on. We tempt them with ideas that we only partially explain. We imply that we're their only source of information. We run out of time so that questions go unanswered. All of these situations are examples of a lack of transparency. In other words, the Scotch tape is starting to really get yellow and it's getting harder and harder to read what's underneath it. Eventually people will stop trying to read what's underneath the yellowing tape!

Somehow we, as educators, have to learn to make our educational programming as transparent as possible. Our objective should be to provide opportunities for the learner to get in touch with the learning resources without having to spend valuable energy in dealing with us - the educator. The learners should be comfortable with us to the extent that they feel empowered to move directly to the learning that they seek. If we get really good at transparent programming the learners may eventually not even notice that we're there.

What a powerful feeling - learning on your own. All it takes is some transparent programming!

3. Apply 2 Gallons Per Acre.
Wait Two Weeks Before Seeding.
And Let Us Say, Amen.

Reflecting on a unique way for learners to
provide feedback during a presentation.

I knew the conference was going to be a bit different. It was concerned with community and economic development. However, the conference organizers had added the phrase "Faith-Based" to the title. It was a conference on faith-based community and economic development. As I had thought about it I realized that it made a lot of sense. Added to the usual group of community/economic development people who would be expected to attend such a conference would be a set of people representing religious organizations that also had a strong commitment to the community and community development. Why not!

I have been familiar with the work of faith-based organizations in the area of community development for many years but it has always been in reference to the developing world. It seems that a large number of the real people-to-people initiatives that go on in the developing world are conducted by non-governmental organizations (or, as they are often referred to, PVOs - Private Voluntary Organizations). And, of the PVOs, many are faith-based.

So here I was, sitting in a session of the conference that was entitled "Building Coalitions." And, the speakers were three Baptist Ministers from the city of Detroit. I thought I knew what to expect but I was certainly surprised at what happened.

The first Minister was young and most energetic. He clearly expressed his concerns about the youth that his church was involved with and proceeded to describe some well thought-through programs that were being offered. He clarified the goals of the programs [Uh-huh], described how they went about identifying the needs of the youth [Yes, Yes], how a variety of responses were being carried out [Yes, Uh- huh], and how he had begun working in conjunction with other churches in the area [Yes, Other churches] - the problem was certainly larger than just his single church [Yes, Yes, A large problem].

After awhile he turned the podium over to the second Minister who continued to share similar stories. The second Minister acknowledged a well known Minister who was not able to be with them at the meeting [Yes, Oh yes]. He started to describe a special program that his church was involved with...

I suddenly realized what was happening. The people who were listening to the presentations of the Ministers were responding as if they were back in Detroit sitting in the church. As points were being made at the front of the room, the people were affirming these very points. Sometimes it was just a muttered agreement [Uh- huh] and at other times the restatement of a phrase or word [Really valuable] or [It really is a problem].

The affirmations of the "conference congregation" had a clear rhythm as they followed what was being said. Never loud enough to disturb the flow of the presentation or others who were listening, the affirmations formed a foundation that seemed to carry along throughout the entire session. I found myself listening intently to both the presenters and the listeners - something I had never done before in my role as an educator! I learned a lot about what was being said and how it was being received.

As I reflect on this phenomenon I'm struck by a number of thoughts. Let me try and share a few of them:

- The affirmations had a noticeable effect on the presenters. As a response was heard from the group the presenter would often stay with the point - restating it, embellishing it, further clarifying the point - rather than moving on to something else. When the room was quiet the presenters seemed to move more quickly through their ideas, almost waiting to hear an affirmation that would let them know that they had hit upon a topic of concern to the audience.

- The audience was involved with the presenter. You could see it in the faces of the group. The listeners were actually participating in what was being said and affirming it to those who were seated around them. And, there was no sense of embarrassment or self-consciousness as it was being done. It seemed very natural and casual. Not forced in any way. But the involvement was quite clear.

- The audience was making their own views known to others in the room. Rather than having to wait until the end of the presentation to show their agreement with the ideas of the presenter, members of the audience were able to affirm the ideas as the ideas were being presented. People in the room knew when others agreed with them. They knew when they were alone in their views. They knew when they were a part of the majority. Yet no one needed to ask for a show of hands.

- The presenters looked for the affirmations from the group while they were presenting - they didn't wait until they were finished. As I watched the presenters I could see the affirmations registering in their eyes, in their body language, in the words they chose to use. I watched one minister close his eyes and continue speaking - hearing the group following his words. He didn't need to look because he knew they were with him. Knowing the group was following was an important thing for the presenter.

What a powerful teaching/learning situation! Gone was the old fashioned idea of learners sitting quietly in their chairs, patiently waiting for the question and answer period. Gone was the uneasy silence that so often accompanies, "Are there any questions?" And, gone was that questioning feeling inside of the presenter who was wondering whether or not the learners were tuned in to what was being said.

I'm not yet sure how I'll integrate these ideas into my own teaching. However, I'm really intrigued with the whole idea and I'll be doing some experimenting. If the learner is allowed to play a more active role during the presentation of information, providing feedback to the presenter and other learners, I think it will make a tremendous improvement in the whole teaching/learning environment! **[Yes, Uh- huh]**

4. Being A Good Facilitator: Knowing When To Throw Away Your Plan

There's nothing so important as a solid plan –
especially if you want to change it.

We've been told over and over again that nothing can replace good planning when it comes to offering an educational program. The message that is communicated to us is that we should take the time to sit down and really plot out exactly what we plan to do and what we expect to achieve. After all, isn't this what good education is all about? Then, when the program is offered it should all flow rather nicely.

This all sounds good, but in reality it doesn't seem to work quite that way. In fact, in more times than not, we seem to have to give up on our plans due to some unexpected event or two that occurs during the program. Maybe too few people show up for the program to divide up into our planned small groups of five. Or, the fantastic slide presentation is discarded when the projector doesn't work. Or, how about the time when that elderly person started off with a very pointed question that changed the direction for the whole evening.

What do we do? It seems that on the one hand we have a case for in-depth planning and on the other hand we have a case for "flying by the seat of our pants." After thinking about this question it would appear there are some basic guidelines that can really help.

- First, there is no replacement for good planning. It should be done completely, in depth and long enough before the event so you can review the plan and know exactly what you plan to do at each point in the program.

- Next, you should share your plan with others, especially those who plan to be in the audience, to see if they feel it will deal with the concerns that the group will have. This is a reality check and should help you avoid some stumbling blocks before they occur.
- Then, when you actually present the program, don't be afraid to change the plan. This demands that you know your plan well enough so that you're comfortable in making changes in it. Learn to listen to the audience, watch for non-verbal cues and other indications that the plan may need revising. Don't be afraid to revise your plan on the spot. There's nothing so frustrating for the audience then to see someone so locked into their plan that they just go right down the drain with it. No one has to know that you're about to change your plan - just do it. Only when we don't know our plan very well do we become overly committed to making it happen in the exact way it was designed.

There is a tremendous chance that the instructional situation that we envision (and use as the basis for our plan) will turn out to be different than the one that we face when we offer the program. No amount of good planning can avoid this. Be prepared for this. Have your plan well learned and then relax to the point that you can be alert to changes that may be needed.

There's nothing so important as a solid plan - especially when it comes to changing it.

5. Make A Left At The Next Light

Creating a learning community that welcomes learners.

At a recent conference the keynote speaker made reference to an ideal community. He described this community as a place that was functioning perfectly in every way. In fact, the people of the community knew each other so well they didn't have any street signs! They didn't need them. Everyone had grown up in the community, knew the community, was comfortable in their interactions with and within the community. Street signs would have been a waste of money.

It was an interesting metaphor. In my own neighborhood I don't know many of the street names but I know where people live. It comes from living in the same place for awhile. When someone says let's go over to the Smith house you just do it. You don't need the help of the signs.

As I continued to think about a community with no street signs a number of other visions came to mind. Probably the most prominent was the vision of an organization or a group that functions so well that it has, using the same metaphor, taken down it's street signs. The people that work in the organization function well. They know where everything is. They know how the organization operates. They clearly know the boundaries of their functioning.

That would be a great organization to work for. Or would it? An experience that I had in Indonesia quickly came to mind:

We lived in Indonesia in the mid 70s. Every six months I was faced with the task of renewing the visas for the family. Recognizing that the government had recently passed a ruling that eliminated charges for visas, I decided to take care of my own visa renewal rather than "paying off" the person who had always done it in the past. I considered myself a logical thinker who could probably get through most any set of hoops that I had to jump through. How hard could it be to get some visas renewed?

I started at the top, thanks to my secretary's husband's second cousin. He headed the key government bureau that was responsible for sanctioning my visa renewal request. It took only a few minutes, a smile and a handshake. His aide applied the official government stamp and then he added his signature. He then showed me the small place on the back of the form that needed only a single additional signature for the process to be complete. He told me exactly where to go for this final signature and bid me farewell. I was 99% finished and I had just begun the process!

I then embarked on a mystery that will forever remain a mystery - because there were no street signs!

The official whose signature was needed on the back of the form wasn't in the office that afternoon. In fact, he wasn't in the office for the next four days. Finally on the fifth day he was there but couldn't sign the form since it had not yet been authorized by the parallel office in another ministry. So, off to the other office. They were happy to sign, however, it would require a disclaimer from the city's office of taxation that showed I owed no back taxes. This seemed logical until I found that as a resident alien I had no dealings with the city tax office - all of my dealings were with the external affairs tax office. So, I proceeded to the external affairs tax office that had never even heard about the form that I needed to have signed. I then returned to the city tax office which was now closed for a three day holiday.

14

I think you know how the rest of the story turns out.

> *Exactly three weeks after I had obtained that very first signature and a handshake my frustration level hit the ceiling. How was it possible that I could spend three weeks - full time - and get no where? I returned to the office of the person who I had previously been "paying off." I quickly counted out the required "payoff" money and asked if it would be possible for him to get my visa renewed. I suggested that he may have to expedite the process since I was almost three weeks late. He had it for me in 2 days!*

Now I think I understand what happened. The government was the same as a community with no street signs. My friend the expediter had "lived in the community" for such a long time that he knew all of the streets. He didn't need any street signs. In fact, the lack of street signs clearly kept him, and a number of others, working very regularly. There was no way you could get your visa renewed without one of these "guides" who knew how to access the community with no street signs.

As educators we can't afford to create communities with no street signs. It's essential that we create street signs, more street signs, and even more street signs that let those who are not part of our educational organization be able to access our resources with ease. Our goal should be to create a learning community with clearly written street signs throughout the community that help people easily move about.

There are a number of ways that we can help in the positioning of street signs in the learning community. When we are speaking to groups we can work hard to use vocabulary that is understandable to all. Our selection of the examples that we use to demonstrate our points can be drawn from experiences that we have all had. We can work hard to not only create ways for people to access our organization, but also ways to easily exit our organization with the needed resources so that they can effortlessly get back to where they were. And, we can work to help people understand how they can become much more effective as self-directing learners in the future.

These ideas and others like them are all forms of positioning street signs in the learning community. A community built on openness and responsiveness. And above all, the ability to easily move about and interact with people and ideas.

6. I've Got An Idea. Let's Have A Program

Looking at the variety of reasons for
designing an educational program.

Ever sit back and think through exactly why you initiate the educational programs you do? Certainly there are those programs that are initiated because of the "needs of the people." However, in addition to responding to people's needs, we've all initiated programs for a variety of other reasons. Let's take a look at some of the many reasons why we initiate programs:

- **Professional expertise** is when we initiate a program based upon some special expertise that we or someone we know has and is willing to share. It's taking advantage of an opportunity. We begin by lining up the expert/resource person and then we work hard to find some people who are interested in learning from this expert. If we really understand the community we serve, we usually know from the beginning whether or not we will find people interested in this expert.
- Different than professional expertise is the development of a program based on **new information** that has become available and needs to be disseminated. As new knowledge becomes available it is important for us to develop programs to get that knowledge appropriately to the people that need it. Developing an educational program for bringing new information to our community is certainly key to our success.
- An "opportunity is knocking" form of program initiation is when we need to **spend available money**. This sounds like a rather weak reason for planning an educational program but

we seem to do it a lot. We immediately pull together one or two others at the office and come up with a quick plan for solving the problem - spending the money before we lose it.

- Of course, the more typical money-related reason for initiating a program is an attempt to **generate income**. When generating income is the driving force behind program development there are two rather difficult, and often arbitrary, decisions that we have to deal with. First, if we decide to take an existing program and change it into a revenue producer, which program do we go with? And, second, how do we establish an appropriate price structure? Do we price the program on its value? Do we price the program on what people are willing to pay? Or, do we price the program on how much revenue we need?

- A **requirement/order/mandate** is another reason why we initiate educational programs. It's when we are "told" that we must offer a certain program. This can be a very difficult situation. Educational programs are usually built around a relationship of trust that we develop with the learners and the community. A problem can easily rise up when there is a potential that such trust may be violated. And, mandates usually have that potential - they emanate from sources other than the people in which we have developed a trusting relationship. It's important when responding to a mandate for program development that we consider how great is the potential to violate the trust we've developed with the learners.

- I hate to mention this one, but we've all seen it (in someone else's program!). It's called **organizational perpetuation** and is programming that is designed to maintain and continue the organization. It serves *our* needs almost exclusively. Of course, it can be argued that at some level we all have to be concerned with organizational perpetuation as part of our role as an educator. I'll let you decide how significant that role should be.

- And finally, the one reason that always seems to make sense is when we initiate programs to **respond to the needs of people**. This is the one that's always referred to in the text books and is often the basis for our programming efforts. The problem with such program development is that the needs of the learners may be very difficult (expensive, awkward, complicated, ever changing, etc.) to deal with.

In looking over this list of reasons why we initiate educational programs I'm sure you can find your own actions in more than one category. This is certainly expected and hardly a problem. The important question to ask is, "What balance have I achieved between these different categories?"

Hopefully the balance that you have achieved between categories is something that you have achieved in a conscious way - rather than having it done "to you." And, when all is said and done, you have been careful to tip the scales in favor of the people you serve. It's fine to initiate programs for all sorts of reasons. When the learner is no longer the basis for initiating educational programs, however, you have lost your foundation and the future is questionable.

7. Learning While Driving

*The power of "sharing" as an essential
strategy for helping adults learn.*

We were cruising past Cleveland heading toward Pittsburgh
when I came out of a minor trance behind the steering wheel. As I
regained full consciousness I started to reflect on the usual sort of
thing - the last 40 miles had flown by and I wasn't even aware of
them. We seem to have this type of revelation fairly regularly
demonstrating how our mind can be a thousand miles away yet the
routine of driving seems to trudge along all by itself. However, it
only took a few seconds of processing before I moved to another
thought.

True, I couldn't tell you a thing that had happened on the
roadway for the past half hour, but I could recount, detail-by-detail,
just about everything said by the correspondent who had been talking
on the radio. My amazement wasn't focused on what I hadn't been
noticing - the road, driving, etc. - but instead it was focused on the
intensity of what I had been listening to on the radio.

The correspondent had just written a book detailing the time
he had spent in Sarajevo working for an independent newspaper
there. He described the heterogeneity of the staff, working side-by-
side, to publish a daily newspaper that attempted to tell the whole
story of the strife of the city. He described how the number of pages
for each day's paper varied depending on the availability of
newsprint that day. Yet, the number of obituary pages was never
compromised since the newspaper served as a major vehicle for
getting out the information about who had been killed in the previous
days. People would come to the newspaper office in a steady stream
each day with scraps of paper that recorded the deaths of family
members and friends. The newspaper recognized their significant

role in maintaining the network for sharing information in the community. They knew that people no longer were able to publicly meet and easily pass information in face-to-face ways. Therefore the newspaper's publishing of death notices took on new significance.

The correspondent described the reporter who had been able to fly out of Sarajevo to attend the presentation of an award for her journalism. However, the reporter carried a sandwich in her pocket rather than eat an elaborate lunch. She didn't want to forget what her colleagues, those who weren't so fortunate to have traveled away from the city, were going through. And, as soon as her commitment was finished, she was on a return flight to Sarajevo to once again face the uncertainty of life in the city.

I could go on and on. I can still remember so much from that broadcast. But why? What was it about the broadcast that was so captivating that it demanded my attention for its entirety? As I thought about this phenomena a number of things came to mind and gained clarity for me.

First of all, I knew that one of the keys to adult learning was that information that related to specific needs that we were faced with were usually learned quite well. However, I had no "need" to learn about Sarajevo. I didn't know anyone from there. I had never visited the city. I had no plans to go there.

I quickly went through the other adult learning essentials. Did it relate to a developmental task that I was facing? No. Was there a concern to immediately apply this information? No. Did it strongly relate to some part of my prior experience? No. Then why was it so captivating?

Finally I pinpointed what had happened. It wasn't me that was the basis for the learning. It was something that the correspondent had done. It became clear then that the correspondent wasn't lecturing to me or the others that were listening that night. Instead he was attempting to share his experiences. His intention was clearly to share that which had made such a strong impression on

22

him. He had spoken with obvious conviction because he wasn't just quoting facts and figures or telling lifeless stories. He was drawing on those experiences that he had in Sarajevo that had the most profound effect on him and was sharing them with the listener. It seemed that his intention wasn't to change anyone or anything. He only wanted an opportunity to share with me that which had been so emotional for him.

And it wasn't just his experiences that he shared. He also shared his thinking and his reflections on those experiences. He shared his very personal thoughts from his time in Sarajevo. He didn't talk like someone who was doling out information. No, it was clear that he "trusted" the radio listener and was willing to share his very private feelings about what he had witnessed.

Now it made a lot more sense. I, the listener, had responded to the correspondent's willingness to trust me with his reflections. And the way in which I had responded was by listening intently and learning! Now, what if we as educators did similarly!

The strategy seems so logical. It we believe in what we're trying to teach to others we should have a batch of experience that helps amplify our ideas. And, if we work at not only sharing these experiences with people in the community (notice, I used the word "sharing" rather than "telling") but also sharing our reflections on these experiences we can help people begin to understand the meaning of what we're trying to teach. And, the framework for all of this must be a sense of trust that the learner has the power and the ability to take that which we share and draw meaning from it.

It all seems so logical. The challenge is to look for ways to do it. Ways to share not only appropriate experiences but also the reflections that we have made on those experiences. And, to trust the listener to draw significant meaning from our sharing. It's worth a try!

8. I Did Everything I Could Think Of To Teach Them. Why Didn't They Learn What I Wanted Them To?

Maybe there's a good reason why someone doesn't want to learn.

Every once in a while we walk away at the end of an educational program/class with a terribly frustrating feeling. No matter what we did to teach during the program the people seemed to be unmoved. Sure, they were courteous and laughed at our jokes, but you could just feel that they really didn't care. When question time came it was like pulling teeth to get anyone to ask anything. Attempts at interaction fell flat. And, after the first few long silences, you worked hard to avoid any further silences. Wasn't learning a two-way street? When were they going to do their part?

Our choices for action following such an event usually fall into two categories. Category #1, known as the "I'll have to work harder next time" category, sounds like this:

> *Oops, the program didn't go so well today. I guess I wasn't quite up to my usual self. I'll have to work harder the next time. Maybe I'll try a few different teaching ideas to get people more involved. I know I can do it if I really try!*

Then, there's Category #2 - the category we assume that we'll never fall into. It's commonly referred to as the "Oh well - who cares" category.

> *Oops, the program didn't go so well today. Well, that's one less I have to do! No point in getting very concerned, there's too many other things on my agenda right now. You win a few - you lose a few!*

Traditional thinking fails to consider that our actions could be guided by something besides these two over-worked categories. Herbert Kohl suggests that there are situations that we educators can find ourselves in when the learner doesn't want to learn - and for good reason! The learner may have consciously or subconsciously decided that there was too much at stake to want to make a change - to want to learn. In other words, the fact that the program seemed to flop was more a function of the learner and his/her desire not to learn than it was a function of our inability to teach.

Kohl, in a delightful short book entitled **I Won't Learn from You!: The Role of Assent in Learning**, says that we, as educators, are sometimes guilty of showing a lack of respect for the learner's "ability to judge what is appropriate learning" for him/herself. We make the assumption that the reason that the learner didn't learn is because of something we did or didn't do. In fact, deciding not to learn may be a purposeful act on the part of the learner. Kohl proposes that the learner's act of not learning can be a very powerful and challenging exercise and require extreme skill on the part of the learner.

> "Learning how not to learn is an intellectual and social challenge; sometimes you have to work very hard at it. It consists of an active, often ingenious, willful rejection of even the most compassionate and well-designed teaching."

So what to do if you're faced with someone who doesn't want to learn? First, begin to understand that refusal to learn is different than failure to learn. A person's refusal to learn may be based on very logical thinking. For instance, a farmer may not want to learn because...

> *If I give up my current farming practices and adopt new practices I will be letting down the generations of my family*

*that preceded me on this farm. I owe it to their memory to
follow in the path that they worked so hard to make for me.
I'm not going to learn these new practices.*

Second, consider strategies that will allow the learner a voice
in making the decision to learn - don't you be the only one making
the decision. The learner has to understand that the act of learning
will be more empowering than the act of not learning! By allowing
the learner a voice in the decision making you're able to demonstrate
the potential to become more empowered - an essential ingredient in
helping a learner overcome a desire not to learn. It's important that
the learner feel that the new learning that is being proposed will lead
to more (and not less) power for him/her.

And third, make sure that your role is separate from what is
to be learned. It should be possible for the learner to be able to talk
about his/her willingness to learn (or not) without a fear that your
feelings will be hurt. Too often the educator and the learning are not
separate, they are combined, and saying "no" to one is the same as
saying "no" to both. The learner should be able to say no to the
learning without feeling that he/she is saying no to the educator. If
we want to help the learner accept new ideas, we must, as the
educator, be able to walk alongside the learner as he/she wrestles
with the decision to learn or not to learn. We must provide a safe
environment for the learner to wrestle with the consequences of
learning or not.

Helping someone learn can mean more than just selecting
the right content and the right teaching strategies. Helping someone
learn can also mean understanding the person's motivations to learn.
We usually make the assumption that everyone wants to learn what
we have to teach. This isn't always the case! When we're faced with
someone who has made a decision not to learn we best search out
new ways to help the person. And, the new ways should be built on
our willingness to walk alongside/with the person.

9. Must They Always Learn Something New?

Instead of "new things", sometimes it's important to relearn old things.

I fell right into the trap when our youngest daughter was in elementary school. We'd all be sitting at the dinner table and I'd casually come up with something like, "What did you learn in school today?" Being a rather bright 4th grader she knew what I was up to and she'd creatively give me an answer which she knew wasn't what I was looking for. Most often she'd shrug off my question with a quick, "Oh, nothing."

Now I mentioned the idea that I fell into a "trap." That's because I think it really is a trap that we sometimes unwittingly hop right into. We seem to assume that unless you've learned something new and are aware of having learned it, then you really haven't gotten your money's worth as a learner. Try as I might, though, I'd continually come up with the same question at the dinner table, "What did you learn in school today?" You'd think I would have gotten a bit smarter after awhile.

A few years back I began to revisit these dinner conversations as I found myself including the very same message on the evaluation forms that I was creating for different workshops that I was designing. It seemed the dinner table was continuing to haunt me.

WORKSHOP EVALUATION FORM

1. Identify one or more strengths of today's workshop.
2. Identify one or more weaknesses of today's workshop.
3. Name 3 new concepts/ideas that you learned during today's workshop.

Egad!! There it was - disguised as number three. It was, quite clearly, the same dinner table conversation of years earlier - "What did you learn in school today?"

I knew from many years as an adult educator that we just don't go about learning new things all the time. In fact, sometimes instead of learning new things we learn old things all over again. So, if I was smart I'd stop using the "new things" paradigm and begin to move toward a "new and old things" paradigm. In addition to asking what new thing was learned I could also ask about the things that the learner already knew that were clarified or reinforced during the program.

It made sense.

However, a colleague of mine recently added another dimension to the "new things and old things" paradigm. He suggested that there was yet a third dimension. There were times when we didn't learn new things and we didn't revisit/relearn old things. Instead, we were challenged to look at a number of things we already knew. And, he went on, we didn't resolve anything - our ideas had been challenged and it would now be up to us, over a period of time, to work to resolve this challenge. In essence it was now a "new things and old things and challenged things" paradigm. The additional question would sound something like, "What challenges to your thinking did you sense from today's program that will take you awhile to resolve?"

I liked the sound of it. It immediately refocused my energies and broadened my horizons as an educator. No longer would I have to continually look at the participants and my success in terms of only the new things that were learned at the program. Now I could also look for instances where the participants had gained clarity for things they already knew and also instances where participants were being challenged to reconsider things that they had previously learned. My next step will be to remember to add all three items to the next evaluation form that I design.

By the way, our youngest daughter isn't at the dinner table this year. She's in college studying overseas. We keep in touch very regularly by email. And you know what, she's learning a lot! Certainly some of it is new things but thank goodness she isn't just learning all new things. A lot of the old stuff we taught her is still working and being reinforced quite nicely in her day-to-day life. And, of course, there's a lot of her that's being challenged - though she isn't sure where it's all leading as of this time.

10. Something Isn't Interesting
Unless Someone's Interested In It.

Motivation to learn lies within the learner - not something that is external and can be manipulated by the educator.

I spotted the title of this paper on the way home the other day. It was clearly lettered on one of those portable signs sitting out in front of a store. I glanced at it as I drove by. I didn't pay a lot of attention to it at the time. It kept popping back into my mind for the rest of the day. I tried to remember the exact wording. I couldn't. After dinner I took a ride. (I made sure I had pencil and paper with me.)

"Something isn't interesting unless someone's interested in it." What a great sign! At first it reminded me of the old, "If a tree falls down in the forest and no one is around, does it make a noise?" I guess I never cared whether or not the tree made a noise. However, I always thought that something could be interesting regardless of whether or not anyone cared.

How many times have I said, "Look at that interesting looking house." Or, "Here's an interesting story." We always assume that something is interesting because of the something. It never occurred to me that it probably isn't interesting unless someone is interested in it! What's interesting to one person may not be interesting to another person.

As my mind began bumping along with this new realization I started to transfer these ideas to the field of education. The natural link was the topic of motivation. It seems like such a clear parallel and helps to clarify an old bias.

I've always had a hard time responding to the person who is looking for a "motivational educational activity." My usual response of, "You can't motivate people. They have to motivate themselves," doesn't always work. But now it made sense to me. All I have to do is rewrite the title. "Something isn't motivating unless someone is motivated by it." It changes the emphasis from the thing to the person. Motivation is a function of people and not things. Therefore, you can't pick out motivational activities for a workshop. What you have to do is to understand what the learners think is motivational and then provide those things!

How simple! Yet, how wise.

Education must be a function of working with people. The more we are able to focus our energies on people - their needs, their concerns, their motivations - the more we are able to help people make changes in their lives. If we try too hard to work on things - our presentation, our plan, our agenda - we run the risk of loosing sight of the people. After all, we're in the people business.

Something isn't interesting unless someone's interested in it. And, something isn't motivating unless someone's motivated by it. It all seems to make sense.

P. S. They changed the sign last week. It now has some new message regarding a special sale on garden tools. I'm not sure that it has any inner meaning this time. I'll have to work on it a bit more.

11. Our Commitment Carries Our Words

Considering the "social contract" that
exists between educator and learner.

Sit back and help me think this one through. I've been pondering the whole idea of how we can improve our instruction with the learners we work with. Yes, I'm familiar with the more typical ideas - use lots of variety in our teaching techniques, provide a good opportunity for questions and answers, if possible break up into small groups for discussion, have appropriate handouts, etc. In fact, I can justly be accused of having passed these ideas on in presentations I've made to more than a few groups of educators! But, I'm not sure that these sorts of techniques provide enough of an answer.

Here is what has been challenging me recently and is still bouncing around in my head. I don't feel that effective teaching is strongly dependent upon what techniques we use. Now I realize this sounds like blasphemy. But, let me explain a bit further.

I can recall numerous examples of when I used great techniques and my teaching was rather mediocre. And, of course, I can also think of times when I was so involved with the learners that I hardly even focused on the techniques I was using, didn't use much of anything as a teaching technique, and the learning that occurred was remarkable.

Aha, you say, he's finally waking up! Yes, I am waking up and I'm beginning to realize more and more that my experiences aren't unique. In fact, I have an idea that you have also had the same sorts of results. Sometimes people don't learn when you've done a great job. And, at other times, you haven't done anything fancy and they learned wonderful things. So, how do you explain it?

Now, before you overload my email account, I realize the usual response. "It's a function of the learner. The learner has the ultimate control over learning and when he/she wants to learn he/she will learn - regardless of what we have done!" That's fine. I buy it. But certainly we must also have some power in the teaching/learning interaction. After all, if we had no power in this thing why are we right in the middle of it?

Okay, you're still with me. See if this makes any sense - it's not a function of technique that helps someone learn, it's a function of the relationship that we have with the learner. That's right, it's a matter of the *relationship* between the educator and the learner. If the relationship between the two of us is a good one - built on commitment and trust - the learner will feel comfortable and willing to allow some change/new learning to occur. In other words, **the level of commitment that exists between the educator and the learner spells the degree to which the learner will exercise his/her desire to learn!**

The key to this is clearly the concept of commitment. Commitment implies some level of mutuality - a contract of sorts between the educator and the learner. When commitment is strong in the teaching/learning setting the learner trusts the educator and doesn't have to wonder what his/her motives are. The learner is comfortable with the educator and doesn't have to worry about being embarrassed. And, the learner feels trusting enough to be willing to temporally suspend old learnings and try out new ones. Commitment is a strong qualitative component to learning and one that creates a learning link between educator and learner. And it is this learning link, built on commitment, that carries our words to the learner.

There, you have it. If we want to help a learner learn new things - to hear our words - we have to consider the amount of commitment that will be required of us. Sometimes the learning doesn't demand much risk on the part of the learner and the degree of commitment we must make is rather low. However, at other times the learner is up against some rather major decisions/changes in life and therefore the potential risk is greatly increased. In these cases our commitment to the learner must be high for learning to take place. And, without commitment there's a good chance that our words will never reach the learner.

So, now it seems that there are a number of questions that we must ask ourselves to provide us with an understanding of the level of commitment we're willing to bring to the teaching/learning situation and to establish the opportunity for our words to reach the leaner.

- Are there certain learners we're more willing to give commitment to? Who are they? Why are we more committed to some than to others?
- Are there certain content areas that we feel so strongly about that they compel us to be willing to commit more to our learners? What are these content areas? Why do we feel so strongly about them?
- Is there a limit to how many learners we can make strong commitments to? How about the other learners? Can we still help them learn if we aren't fully committed to them?
- What happens when we over commit to a group of learners? Do we then cross over the line and loose our identity as an educator and become one in the same with our learners? Do we risk becoming politicized when we become over-committed to a group of learners?
- How can we tell when the learner recognizes the level of commitment that we're trying to extend? What if the learner fails to recognize our willingness to make a commitment?

And finally the real hard question for me. If commitment is really the key to facilitating learning, how come I had to sit through all those teaching methods classes?

12. Time To Put Away The Book And Do Some Reading

Many answers to problems can be as
close as the world around us.

Paulo Freire, the noted Brazilian educator and revolutionary, was speaking in Ann Arbor a few years ago and made what at first sounded like a rather preposterous statement. He came out and bluntly announced that "infants can read." (Paulo Freire was certainly the master of oration - this comment immediately got everyone's attention!) He then went on to clarify what he meant. He suggested that what it was that the infant could read was the "world" and the infant started doing it at a very early age. The infant, without any formal teaching, could understand much of the surrounding world.

Now that Freire had our attention he continued with his reading metaphor. He suggested that as the infant grew into childhood there came a time when reading the world directly through experience with the world was no longer good enough. In fact, the direct reading of the world eventually was replaced with the need to indirectly read the world. The child was now required to decode a bunch of signs and symbols that represented words that, in turn, represented the world. Reading now became a matter of interpreting words that, in turn, led us to the world.

Freire pointed out that this stepping away from directly reading the world wasn't necessarily bad as long as we could keep everything in perspective and realize that the world was still there, ready to be read in a direct manner, whenever we wanted. He said that the problem arose when the child was taught to become absolutely reliant on the indirect world, disciplined to only read words and sentences, and to distrust the real world. In fact, the child who would excel at reading the signs and the symbols would be highly rewarded - would advance in school, would find new opportunities available, would receive recognition. On the other hand, the child who delighted in reading the real world, who was slow to learn indirect reading through the decoding of signs and symbols, was frowned upon and made to feel inferior.

Freire suggested that the assumption that accompanied the requirement of learning to read words and sentences was that it would allow us to better communicate with each other about the real world. We could write stories about the world, document occurrences in the world, or project events that might occur in the world. However, the failure in the system seemed to be that once started on the path of reading words and sentences, the child never really returned to reading the world in its direct and real form. The child developed a dependence on the printed word and not the world. Reality was now removed to the printed word.

Let's take Freire's view of "reading" and bring it to bear on our role as an educator. It is essential that the educator have a firm grasp on understanding the difference between reading the world and reading the words and sentences that we create to describe the world. Though both forms of reading are essential, we tend to sometimes forget about direct reading of the world.

Often the problems that are brought to the educator can be solved in quick order if the learner went back to reading the world - looking for ideas and solutions to the problem, not in what has been written about the problem, but by directly experiencing the problem and possible solutions to it. In addition, the learner must reflect back on those previous times of direct experience that can provide additional insight into the problem. The key to learning can often be the direct reading of situations and problems that occur around us and then the further reading of ways to resolve the problems.

Reading the world would seem to demand certain strengths that can be developed and reinforced by the educator.

- First, reading the world suggests keen perception. It's the ability to use our senses to truly see the problem and what surrounds the problem.
- Second, reading the world must be built on inquisitiveness. We must embody a spirit of inquiry and examination that draws us further into the world.
- And finally, reading the world must draw on reflection. We must look at the reality and reflect on it in terms of the many and varied experiences that we've had in the world.

Given this approach to "reading" I think it's possible for us as educators to make very positive strides in helping people solve the problems they are facing. And, we can do it by helping people return to reading that which they first started reading - the world. Reading the world is often the basis for empowerment - especially for those who tend to become dependent upon others when forced to only read words and sentences.

13. Half Empty Or Half Full?

The challenge is to view the learner as being "half full" rather than "half empty."

I'm sure you're familiar with that old adage about the glass being half empty or half full. You know, it's the one where you attempt to describe a person's approach to something as either a positive or negative one. If a person is approaching an issue as if the glass is half full, the issue is being approached in a positive way. Conversely, if the issue is being approached in a negative way it is being dealt with by a person who sees the glass as being half empty.

This half empty/half full saying seems to date back in my mind to the beginning days of undergraduate study. Those were the days when we stayed up all night discussing these huge and very complex issues until somehow we resolved the issues and had "the answer." Of course, after a bit of sleep, the answer had once again disappeared. I remember working out elaborate schemas for why there were no absolute answers in the world (and on other nights how there were absolute answers for everything in the world), what would happen to the world if there was no concept of war, and whether or not it was possible to ever print a googolplex (a googol is a "1" followed by 100 zeroes; a googolplex is a googol to the googol power - a very large number.).

I thought I was pretty well finished with these cute sayings and mind puzzles until recently when I revisited the half empty/half full saying once again. As you can expect I managed to add a new element to the old adage. This time my reflections were guided by my concerns for education and the values that each of us brought to the teaching situation. I was pleased to find that the half empty/half full idea helped me clarify why it seemed that some people were so very powerful in their teaching and others weren't. Let me explain -

It seems that the educator has a choice to view the learner as someone who doesn't know something, or as someone who does know something. (There's the half empty/half full dichotomy.)

The educator who begins by looking for what the learner doesn't know (the half empty view) begins teaching by first spending time doing a learning needs assessment - finding out what the learner doesn't know. In fact, for many educators this is absolutely the place where you must start. You must find out what the learner doesn't know so that you can then go about filling the void.

On the other hand, the educator who begins by trying to better understand what the learner does know (the half full view) begins by getting a sense of what strengths the learner is bringing to the instructional setting. In other words, what is the foundation that the learner has already developed that can serve as a building block for the instruction? What does the learner already know?

As I continued to consider these opposing views I wondered if the difference was merely a matter of semantics. However, as I looked closer it became apparent that there really was a major difference. And, the difference was easiest seen from the view of the learner - not the educator. The learner who is treated as if he/she doesn't know something gets off to an entirely different start than the learner who is treated as if he/she does know something.

And, given the choice of how I would like to be treated as a learner I would clearly choose to be treated as someone who does know something - a half full learner who is on his way to becoming more full.

44

14. There's A Learner In Each Us (Hopefully!)

We learn the best from teachers
who are good learners.

As I reflect on those educators that have had a strong effect on my own learning I keep coming to the same conclusion, "Each of the educators that have strongly influenced me have also been good learners themselves."

Here's what I mean. I remember taking clarinet lessons in college from Mr. Stein. Mr. Stein was an outstanding teacher. He got me to understand abstract musical concepts that I had never been aware of before. It seemed that he had the power to open new insights for me at every turn. He was excited with what he believed in and got me to be excited with my own abilities at music. He listened to me. He heard me. He even learned from me!

Mr. Stein would describe to me things that he had recently learned and his descriptions would always be accompanied by a certain childish excitement as if discovering a new play toy for the first time. He looked about himself to learn things in a variety of different places. He would look in those places where previously he had seen nothing and this time he'd delight in finding something that had been there all along but had gone unnoticed. He was constantly looking to learn. And when he learned something he wasn't content to just "sit on it," he had to share it with someone else - his students.

This remembrance still burns in my mind. And why? Because I have always considered Mr. Stein one of my most influential teachers. And now as I think back it becomes more clear. He was a good teacher because he was a good learner.

It seems to be so much easier to learn from a learner. Rather than feeling like a "lowly" student you are elevated to a co-learner/co-teacher level that is most exciting. There was always a sense of reciprocity when you were with Mr. Stein. It was like a two way street with each of us learning from each other.

So what can we learn from understanding that Mr. Stein was a good teacher because he was a good learner? First, take time to make sure that we're still learning. Notice that when we aren't doing much learning the days seem to get a lot longer and the work seems to carry little excitement for us. Next, we must look around to see if and what others are learning. If they aren't doing so well, maybe a little help is needed. One way to help is just to show them that learning can be exciting - maybe they forgot. And finally, we have to try to be reciprocal as an educator by providing opportunities for others to teach us. It doesn't have to be formal teaching. Just a clear indication that we're learning from them.

As an educator we carry some extra "baggage" when it comes to being a learner. It seems that only through our ability to learn from others can we become more secure so that others will learn the important messages we have for them. By modeling good learning techniques and excitement for learning we begin to establish an expectation in others that we hope that they too will learn. It's the learner in each of us that empowers us to move forward as the educator we'd like to be.

15. Reflecting To Learn And Learning To Reflect

The essential role that reflection
plays when learning new things.

Learning has always been a rather intriguing topic for me. That is, of course, until I have to explain it to someone else. Whenever forced to explain "What do you mean by learning?" I tend to get a bit too technical and turn a dynamic concept - learning - into just another technical topic. Certainly there's a better way to describe "learning" than speaking of it as "A change in a person's behavior." But what?

The first step in trying to define learning is to make sure we understand the difference between teaching and learning. Teaching is something that we, as educators, do and it often results in learning. However, there is no guarantee that teaching will always result in learning. In fact we're all too familiar with a lot of teaching we've sat through where learning was not an outcome!

The difference is that teaching is a function of the educator/teacher and learning is a function of the learner. As we try to define learning we must make sure that we focus our attention on the learner and not the teacher.

Okay, so let's look inside of ourselves as learners to better understand the concept of learning. What is it that I do that seems to result in learning? The answer is now more clear. It seems that what I do to help with learning is to ponder, to contemplate, to question, to consider, and to examine. These are all aspects of reflection.

When I want to learn I reflect. I reflect on what I've been seeing. I reflect on what I've been hearing. I reflect on any number of things. Sometimes my reflections result in new understandings - that's learning. At other times my reflections don't quite resolve with anything and I end up with just a bunch of additional questions. At these times I sense I haven't yet learned. But no hurry. I'm sure I'll revisit the topic if it's important to me. And, maybe the next time my reflections will yield new understanding and I'll have learned something new.

As I've come to understand the concept of reflection as a key to learning it has also become clear that the way I test my reflection is to act on it. Once I've reflected and come up with a new chunk of learning I then go out and do something based upon my new learning. And, of course, the putting of my reflection into practice gives me all sorts of feedback that I can then further reflect on. It's a very dynamic process that seems to be going all the time. I'm continually reflecting and acting and reflecting and acting and... Sometimes I feel like I'm starting the process at the acting stage and will do my reflecting later. At other times I sense that I'm doing the reflecting first and will probably act on it later - once I have a good idea of what my actions should be.

Now I don't think I'm very unique. I look around me and see others doing the same thing. I see a farmer looking over his records to reflect on prior years before moving toward a decision regarding how he will approach his task for this year. I think he's learning. I see a Township Supervisor talking over coffee with local people to get a better sense of local concerns. I think there's learning going on. I see medical personnel in the emergency room at the hospital discussing a particularly puzzling case. They're trying to learn. And for all of them, whatever they're about to do is certain to be influenced by their reflection. And after they finish doing their task, they'll probably be back reflecting again to see what they might do differently the next time. I think this is what learning is.

So now that I've defined it, what can we do to make it happen more consistently? In other words, how can we learn to reflect?

- If we're working with a group of people the easiest way is to just begin by saying something like "Let's talk about what we just did." Or, challenging people with a question such as "Why do you think that's the best answer?" or "Are there other ways to solve the problem?"
- Reflection works best when the atmosphere is very open and there isn't a feeling that we have to come up with the "right" answer. There is opportunity to hear all sides and equal treatment is given to a variety of views. The educator is more a facilitator of discussion than a deliverer of information.
- It's important during reflection to move back and forth between identifying specific things that have just happened and then trying to reflect on them. Sometimes we end up reflecting on our reflections and it gets a bit too fuzzy!
- When it seems time to draw reflection to a close it often is very helpful to turn our attention to what will come next. Reflection of the best type is always followed by action of some sort. Rather than leaving a group in the middle of reflection, always allow time to discuss what sorts of actions people may now be willing to take to gain further insight on their reflections. What will we now be doing? What will I be trying to do that might be a bit different because of my reflection?
- And finally, it's always helpful to finish up with some clear understanding of when and how people will again have an opportunity to do some further reflecting. It might mean another group meeting to share and discuss (reflect on) what has happened since we last talked. Or, it may mean the development of a short list of questions that people can bring home with them to stimulate their own individual reflection. Reflecting is how we learn and it is possible to help people to learn to reflect.

16. Unanticipated Learning

Sometimes it's impossible to know ahead of time what people might be learning from your programs.

A long time ago I learned that a smart educator should always be concerned about unanticipated learning. You know, the kind of learning you hadn't realized was going to occur from the program you just offered.

I found that by talking about unanticipated learning as a key type of learning for adults it could get me out of all sorts of trouble. It allowed me to stand up and proudly take credit for learning that, in my wildest dreams, I would never have predicted would have occurred.

> **Learner:** *"Hey Joe, that was a tremendous session you just facilitated. I not only learned about the topic of the program but I also had a conversation with Fred Smith and, would you believe it, I found out that..."*
>
> **Joe:** *"Glad to hear that you enjoyed the session. You know, since unanticipated learning is so important to us adults, we made sure that when we planned the program we provided opportunities for..."* (Who was I kidding?)

I was getting so good at these responses that after awhile I began to believe my own words! Unanticipated learning was the answer for everything. It was as good as motherhood and apple pie since unanticipated learning was driven by learner needs rather than instructional objectives. Unanticipated learning was problem focused. Unanticipated learning was immediate. Wow, it sounded so good.

But wait a minute. Why was I taking credit for something that is so clearly a function of the learner - and not the educator? Plus, what is unanticipated learning? Is it as good as I thought? Or, is it merely a learner compensation for my shortcomings?

Recently I got some answers that have helped clear up my thinking. Here's what I've found:

- First, unanticipated learning usually occurs as a function of dialogue and interaction. It's really hard for unanticipated learning to occur when a learner is off working alone. When a learner is sharing ideas and thoughts with other learners, exchanging views on a topic, the opportunity for unanticipated learning is high.
- Second, most learners don't enter into a learning situation expecting to bump into some unanticipated learning. They usually enter the learning situation with a clear goal in mind. And, it is on the way toward that goal that unplanned learning takes place.
- Third, most unanticipated learning occurs at a very significant level of meaning for the learner. It isn't the superficial type of learning. Instead it's the type of learning that is usually accompanied by an "Aha."
- And fourth, unanticipated learning usually occurs in response to a learning need that may have been lurking just below the surface for the learner. The learner doesn't always realize that it's lurking there but when an answer to that lurking need presents itself - Shazam! - unanticipated learning!

When I reflect on unanticipated learning I get my best view when I think of myself as the learner (not the educator). As a learner I find all of the above points really make sense. In fact, as a learner, I often enter into a learning situation hoping that unanticipated learning will take place.

I wonder how many others do the same thing. I wonder how many of the people attending my educational programs are hoping that I've structured the program in such a way that unanticipated learning can occur.

Sometimes I find myself wondering if it's possible to move unanticipated learning into the realm of anticipated learning. But I usually catch myself. I don't think the learner inside of me wants to give up the excitement that accompanies unanticipated learning. I guess I need some dialogue to help me think this through. I think I'll go find someone to talk to about this idea. Or, maybe I can write a short essay...

17. To Begin Or To End: That Might Be The Question

Building on the Carl Rogers concept that we don't learn from conclusions.

I've been accused (over and over again) of being too much of a starter. I'm always interested in beginning things but it seems that I don't have nearly the interest in finishing things. I've always viewed this as a function of my not needing much closure. The challenge for me seems to be at the front end of an activity - how to get the activity going. I'm challenged with the whole process of setting something in motion. Once set in motion, though, I move on to something else.

I'm sharing this because I could name a whole bunch of people I drive crazy because of this behavior. Until recently my reaction to these people has been one of avoidance - if I can ignore them they'll probably go away!

However, this all changed after my last rereading of Carl Rogers' book **Freedom to Learn**. I've always liked Rogers but now I have new admiration for him. He's given me a rationale for why it's better to begin things rather than to end things. Thanks Carl!

Rogers, reflecting on how we go about teaching and learning, suggests that we don't learn from conclusions. Instead he says that we learn through actual experience. What he's concerned about is the rather standard approach to education whereby the teacher spends the greatest amount of time talking to the learners and presenting conclusion after conclusion to them. It's almost as if the teacher has become an attorney making an argument before a court. Such teaching, according to Rogers, is founded on the false premise that we can actually learn from all of these conclusions as they are being thrown at us.

To the contrary, Rogers says that we learn best through self-appropriated learning and not through conclusions. We learn best by going out and directly experiencing things and then drawing meaning or conclusions of our own from the experience that we've had. The role of the teacher, in Carl Rogers' view, would be better invested in helping learners go about identifying the sorts of experiences that they would like to learn from and then helping them become involved in those experiences.

To clarify this idea, think of the times you've been somewhere or done something and then tried to share it with someone who wasn't there. It usually flops in the retelling of the adventure. It doesn't have the same meaning to the person who wasn't there. For you, it had tremendous meaning because it was a self-appropriated experience/learning. For the other person it turns into an exercise whereby all they get to hear is the description of some events and the inevitable conclusion of what happened to you. No fun for them.

With this as background, Rogers goes even further in his clarifying of good education. "We don't learn from conclusions, we only learn from beginnings." Certainly it makes sense. Conclusions are those things that someone else has experienced and then they are brought to us, without the benefit of the experience to learn from. Beginnings are the things that we ourselves experience and form the basis for our own conclusions.

Now I feel better. My avoidance of closure and my desire to always begin things (and seldom finish them) is the way learning is supposed to be. By being a perpetual starter I have the benefit of learning lots and lots of things because of all of the experiences I'm having.

Now if I can only get my wife to understand that I've already experienced window washing. I've drawn learning from the experience, and it's time to move on to something else. Somehow I don't think she's convinced that this is what Rogers was referring to.

18. Expressive And Receptive Communication

Arguing for the creation of a balance between teaching learners and learning from learners.

Speech pathologists have long used a pair of concepts to help in describing and remediating communication problems of people. These two concepts, expressive communication and receptive communication, refer to a person's ability to "send" a message to another person and to "receive" a message from another person. Most of us operate using both concepts simultaneously. We receive and we express at the same time. However, a child with an attention deficit may be able to express him/herself quite well, but not be able to sit still long enough to receive communication. On the other hand, a person who has had a stroke may still be receiving communications quite well, but not be able to express him/herself due to a loss of speech.

The other day these concepts were running through my head when it occurred to me that we, as adult educators, are also in the receptive and expressive communication arena. In fact, our success as an adult educator is often dependent upon our ability to keep both of these communication channels in balance for ourself. And, we often experience lots of frustration when they get out of balance.

Standing in front of a group of eager learners often appeals to our expressive communication side. We spend a lot of time presenting to the learners, sharing our ideas, telling them how to do something better, and generally voicing our views of the situation. The expressive side of being an educator is what we often feel we are paid to do. And sometimes we find ourselves thinking that if we didn't do as much expressing we might not be doing our job very well!

However, the receptive side of our educator role must be remembered and encouraged. It is through our ability to be a receptive communicator that we find out what our learners want to know, what they may already know, and whether or not what we may be about to express is worth saying. If anything ever needs improving it is usually the further development of our receptive skills. And to complicate matters, it's not easy to see our receptive skills in action! They operate without making any noise, without causing any attention, and without disturbing the learning environment.

Often it is through the use of our receptive skills that we find out that the ideas we are about to express aren't really what's being asked for. By using our receptive skills in an ongoing and viable manner we are able to better understand the learning needs of our learners and without even constructing a single questionnaire.

Of course, you may be the best receptive communicator in the world, but what do you do if you're working with learners who aren't very expressive. It is then important for us to help the learners become more expressive. The role of the learner is so very similar to the role of the educator in that both expressive and receptive communication must be practiced. Gone is the view that the learner is there only to receive and the educator is there only to express.

By creating a balance between our expressive communication ability and our receptive communication ability we are better able to see needs as they are occurring and respond appropriately. And, to help our learners also understand the distinction between the two and improve the balance between them can spell success on an ongoing basis.

19. Writing An Evaluation Report: Drudgery Or Challenge?

A number of specific strategies for making the writing of an evaluation report less of a drudgery.

Few things evoke as much annoyance, frustration and hostile behavior as the suggestion that you have to prepare an evaluation report. I've seen quiet, mild-mannered folks turn into rather ornery human beings at the very thought that it's now time to sit down and prepare a written document that describes the outcomes of an educational project or program that they have recently conducted.

Of course I realize the negative reaction is often a function of the individual not having collected any data at the event. Oops. Big mistake! It's next to impossible to prepare an evaluation report if you've got nothing to report. We'll dismiss this type of person for now and hope that he/she repents for this sin and gets better in the future about remembering to collect meaningful information surrounding the outcomes of the next program.

Let's, instead, move our focus to the person who has collected information but doesn't really know what to do with it. Here are some suggestions that I hope might save hours of needless hair pulling and begin to move us toward more effective communication of our efforts through the evaluation reports we prepare.

- The last section of your evaluation report will most likely be a summary and recommendations. **After you've written this last section why not move it to the front of your report.** That's right, begin your report with the conclusions/ recommendations. The busy people of the world, those who only have a few minutes to devote to reading your report, will then have the important stuff right at the very beginning. You've greatly enhanced your chances of someone actually reading your report and leaving with the understanding that you'd like them to leave with.

- **Keep your evaluation report short and to the point.** There's no real need to make your evaluation report look like a journal article - especially if you want others to read it.

- **Have a specific audience in mind who will be reading your report** (parent group, colleagues, administrators, a funding agency, etc.) **and write specifically for them.** Don't try to write for too many groups in the same report. Keep it focused and informative.

- **Use quotations of people/participants if at all possible** (and appropriate). This gives life to your data/report. It turns your numbers into something that makes sense and brings a sense of reality to the reader.

- **Make real recommendations.** Don't leave it to the reader to try and figure out what all of your data mean. After you've presented the outcomes of your program move on to draw specific implications and next steps that clearly show the reader how the program you're evaluating can link together with other events to make a significant impact.

- **Create the tables for your report first.** Then, write around the tables - sort of fill in the spaces between the tables with a narrative that describes what the reader is seeing in the tables. Too often we assume that the reader sees the same thing in the tables that we see. ("It's so obvious, I can't believe you drew such a weird conclusion from my data!") A handy rule of thumb when writing an evaluation report is to a) write a short section to introduce the table, b) present the actual table, and c) write a short section to tell what the table means/says.

- **Your evaluation report should help to make your evaluation replicable** - so that someone else can do the same evaluation if they'd like (or, you can repeat the same evaluation next time). Include a copy of the actual evaluation instrument that you used for collecting the data that is described in your report.
- **Put your name on the evaluation report.** If you've done the work, take credit for it. It's also helpful to include an address and phone number. You'd be surprised how the validity of an evaluation report is increased when the author is willing to identify himself/herself.
- If you find an evaluation report prepared by someone else that you really like (from a journal, at a seminar, etc.) keep a copy handy and **model your report after the one you like**. So often the preparation of an evaluation report is hampered because we really don't know the pieces that have to go into the report. Having a model of one that you like can clarify exactly what you will and will not include in your own report and the sequence in which you'll be presenting your findings.

Well, there you have it. A small handful of ideas on how you can prepare an evaluation report without having to pay a best friend to hold a gun to your head until it's done. And, what about that person I mentioned at the beginning of this paper who hadn't collected any data? Now there's no excuse – next time be prepared to document what you have done, collect some information about the program, so you can write an evaluation report. As I've suggested, they're not so bad if you are organized in what you do.

20. The Day Of Presentations

What goes into making a good presentation?

Last summer's Nonformal Education Institute has been over for a couple of months and it is now drifting from my short term memory bin into my long term memory bin. And, of course, as it drifts it looses lots of the specific details and clarity. As I tried to remember some of the more important things that went on in the Institute (before they drifted out of my long term memory bin and into oblivion) I settled on the day of presentations. Imagine - sixteen 15 minute presentations from sixteen different presenters, one after another, on topics ranging from rubber tree plantations in Malaysia to the changing paradigms in China to training youth volunteers in Detroit. And, all of this in one continuous stream with two short coffee breaks and time out for lunch.

As this day of presentations went from presenter to presenter it became very easy to spot the uniqueness in each person's presentation style and to identify those aspects of particular presentations that gave them a special quality. As I observed each presentation I began to note what these aspects were.

- **Provide a beginning overview of your presentation.** This was important to help others know what was about to be presented. It was like a program at a concert. It meant that you as a listener knew when it was time to ask questions, when an activity would start, and when you were nearing the end. It gave you an overall view of the presentation right at the very beginning and helped make you a part of it.
- **"Share with" your audience rather than "talk to" your audience.** Nervousness had some presenters reading their ideas from a script. However, the presenters that chose to sit

back and take an attitude of sharing - allowing the audience to move in step with them - had us all eating out of their hand.

- **Use humor to create a sharing atmosphere.** The best presentations seemed to make use of humor that was related to the topic at hand and poked some fun at the presenter (not at the audience). It made topic and presenter more human.
- **Minimize the use of instructional aids.** The instructional aids of the powerful presentations focused your attention on the presenter – they didn't focus your attention on the instructional aid. They were unobtrusive in nature and never got in the way of the presenter's words. The instructional aids clarified the ideas - they didn't present the ideas.
- **Use a visual presentation to anchor your verbal presentation.** A map, a few key words, or a simple flowchart when projected on the overhead projector seemed to give the presenter something to talk around. The visual had just a few key ideas (not the entire script) and reduced nervousness as it provided the presenter with a sense of security. It also provided us listeners with a place to focus our visual attention.
- **Be able to move from the "teller role" to the "listener role."** Those presentations that were most involving of the audience had the available time split in the middle with only the first half of the time used for lecturing to the group. The second half of the time had the presenter doing a lot of listening and often asking the audience for their opinions or views of what had been presented.
- **Maintain the forward progress of your presentation - don't bog down.** We had an impartial timekeeper, sitting toward the front, who held up small signs indicating to the presenter how much of the 15 minutes remained. The final

TIME IS UP sign was on a bright colored paper for all to see. It helped keep things moving forward.

- **Under-structure the presentation.** Why do we always plan 30 minutes of stuff for a 15 minute presentation? Those presenters who only planned 10 minutes worth were pleasantly surprised when they not only got all of their information presented but also had time left to respond to questions, review key ideas and reinforce the important concepts. This also allowed the group to pull the presentation in directions they felt were important.

- **Demonstrate a technique rather than talking about the technique.** Presenting information about organizing youth activities? Organize the audience and show them how it's done. Explaining a system for assessing learner's needs? Hand out the assessment form and have the audience assess each other's needs. Allowing the audience to experience what you're presenting is much more powerful than merely describing it.

Typically a day of presentations can be a terrible thing to experience. But not this time.

This time it was different. We got through the day in fine order. Every presentation had a message and we all worked to clearly hear these messages. The day of presentations took the participants on a ride that started with commitment to a topic and ended with commitment to each other. We listened to each other. We questioned each other. We learned from each other. And when the day was over we had grown to understand each other and our topic in new and insightful ways. And no one got bored. You never do when you're learning about and from each other.

21. I think I Would Have Paid More Attention If I knew I Was Going To Forget

Knowing what is important to be learned.

Wouldn't it be great if, as we are sitting in a class and being told some bit of information, a small sign would appear and it would tell us if this was something we should remember for the future! Imagine the scene:

Here we are attending some highly touted seminar on one of today's catch phrases. You know the type of program. Successful Approaches to Effectively _____ (fill in your own words). The keynote speaker is up front droning on and on with his prepared presentation. To my left are some colleagues busily taking notes on every word out of the presenter's mouth. I'm starting to feel a bit guilty about not taking my own notes when I spot the sign. There it is! About three feet over his head is a blinking neon sign that says:

**Don't bother remembering this stuff.
You'll never need it!**

Wow! That would be fantastic. I could become so much more efficient in how I invest my time. Sure, I'd carry a notebook with me at all times. However, I wouldn't pull it out until the other neon sign would appear:

**This is what you'll be needing in the future.
Better remember it!**

If only learning were so simple!

Okay, enough dreaming. It'll never happen. Or, as our ancestors can attest, when it happens we'll probably be too old to really care any more.

What options do we have as we proceed head first into the information explosion that surrounds us on all sides these days? How do we know which things are important to remember and which things aren't?

Or better yet, how do we approach the learners we're working with in terms of this question? Should they remember everything we say? Do we have the insight to tell them what to remember and what not to remember? If they shouldn't remember what we're saying, then why are we saying it?

Clearly, there's no easy way to respond to these questions. And the reason is that learning is significantly guided by our past experiences and our abilities to use those experiences to shape our future.

As an educator we have a responsibility to help our learners link what we are saying to their experiences. We must be able and willing to allow the experiences of our learners to significantly enter into the teaching setting and affect that which we're trying to teach. It's only after the learner's experiences are appropriately recognized and built upon that we (and the learners) will begin to be able to deal with the concern about what to learn and what not to learn - what to remember and what to forget.

By helping the learner bring his/her experiences into the teaching setting we're helping the learner better know where attention should be paid. In fact, by helping the learner bring his/her experiences into the teaching setting we're helping the learner create his/her own blinking neon sign!

This material makes sense in
terms of your own experiences.
Better remember it!

22. Strategies For Teaching Adults

*Using teaching strategies that are drawn
from an understanding of adult learning.*

"What's the best way to teach a group of adult learners?" A
question we've heard often but a question that seems to seldom get a
good answer. One person describes a simulation activity as the "best"
while another suggests using a small group activity. Still another
person feels that information is best delivered via a solid lecture.
("After all, we must be sensitive to the time we spend in teaching.
Can we afford to waste the learner's time just to make the activity
more fun?")

How, then, do we answer the question? Is it okay to just say that
there are a lot of different ways for teaching adults? Or, there's no
best way? Here are a few answers:

- First of all, there are multiple ways for teaching adults.
  Different educators and different learners prefer to teach
  and/or learn in different ways. There is no single right way
  to teach. In fact, all of us can and do learn through a variety
  of methods. Looking for the single best way to teach adults
  may be a futile search.
- Second, the one thing we know is that the more participation
  there is from the learner in the planning of the teaching the
  greater the likelihood that good learning will occur. This
  proves true for a lot of reasons. Obviously the learner is able
  to influence our selection of teaching topic and teaching
  process if he/she is involved in the planning. But more
  importantly, the learner, if involved in the planning,
  develops a more realistic expectation of what's about to
  happen in the teaching. That's a good thing to remember -

there's a much greater chance of the learner learning what we're presenting if the learner knows ahead of time what to expect!

- Third, it's not so much what method we use to teach that's important, it's the intentions that we communicate through our teaching that speak the loudest. In other words, a well intentioned educator can use most any technique and have learning as a product. But what are the intentions of a good educator? The intentions of a good educator are wrapped up in the assumptions we make about the people we're teaching. If we assume that we're teaching highly self-directed people then we will use methods that don't create dependence on us. If we assume that the people we're teaching are facing problems in their lives we'll probably make sure we know what those problems are and focus our teaching on them. If we assume that the people we're teaching are creative and like to build their own answers to problems we'll make sure we don't tell them everything but give them an opportunity to build answers that include their own creative touch. Or, if we assume that the people we're working with have many of their own answers we will search out ways to have people work together to help each other in defining answers to problems.

- Finally, don't assume that a one-shot teaching session will do a lot. Certainly there are many instances when we're able to hit the nail on the head and do real good with a single teaching session. However, the odds of this consistently happening aren't very good. The way to insure success is not to limit our teaching to a single session. Work instead on the developing of relationships with learners and create multiple opportunities for working with groups of learners. Through a longer term commitment to a group of learners we will have a chance of really understanding what their learning needs are and whether or not we are helping with the resolution of those needs.

So, what's the best way to teach a group of learners? Your way!! As long as you keep in mind some of the above.

23. Solving Problems Or Posing Problems –
What's Our Role?

*The role of the educator can be seen as
posing problems rather than solving problems.*

When I ran into these two phrases - **problem solving
education** and **problem posing education** - I thought it was sort of a
semantic game. What difference did it make if I were working with
learners to solve problems or to pose problems? The key seemed to
be that my teaching was problem based. Then I got a little cocky and
started thinking that, in fact, it made the most sense if I were in the
problem solving business. What good was it to merely pose
problems? Certainly the learners were looking for answers to their
problems. And my role, therefore, made the most sense if it were the
solving of their problems.

Oops!! A huge hole in the ground just swallowed me up.

How could I possibly solve someone else's problems? Yes,
of course, I could provide some ideas and thoughts that the other
person might employ in the solving of their problems. But, it
wouldn't be me that solved their problems. It would be the learner
solving his/her own problems with the use of my information. After
all I'm an educator and my business is in teaching people how to
solve their own problems - not solving their problems for them.
(Maybe if I were a banker I'd be more successful at solving people's
problems. Any time I'd hear about someone with a problem I'd just
drop a bit of money on it and it would disappear. It would probably
last as long as my money lasted!)

So, if I'm not destined to be a problem solver in my role as
an educator then what am I supposed to do with all of those problems
that are floating around?

Paulo Freire, the Brazilian educator, suggests that a more powerful role for me would be to get into the business of working with learners through problem *posing*. Rather than trying to figure out how a person can solve his/her problem, it makes more sense to work to help the learner better understand exactly what the problem is. I guess it makes good sense that if a person doesn't understand what their problem is there's really not much likelihood that they will ever solve it. And, if they don't understand what the problem is there's even less likelihood that hearing the suggestions of how someone else thinks it should be solved will make any difference!

Helping someone to better understand exactly what the problem is that they are facing often is enough to significantly move the person ahead toward a solution. How many times have we been absolutely stymied over something with no solution in sight until someone helped us redefine the problem in a new way. All of a sudden the problem became so much more understandable and manageable. And, we no longer needed the person to help us solve the problem. We now had a clear enough understanding of the problem that the viable paths toward a solution became so very obvious to us.

In problem posing education the role of the educator moves away from trying to solve the problems of learners and moves toward helping the learners understand the problems they are facing. This can often be accomplished in a variety of ways.

If the learner is understanding the problem that he/she is facing than it might be most appropriate to move right ahead and suggest ways that the problem could be solved. In other words, offering the learner solutions that he/she might consider for solving the problem. (Remember, it's the learner that's going to do the problem solving - not you!)

However, when the learner needs help to better understand the problem they are facing, one of the more powerful ways is through the posing of problems that in one way or another relate to the learner. And then, asking the learner for ideas on how the problems that are being posed can be solved. The learner is put in the driver's seat and is the key person to work on the solution to the problems.

It's important during this process that the educator maintain perspective of the situation and provide appropriate feedback to the learner on his/her dealing with the problem. Freire even suggests that the educator should be constantly looking for new ways to repose the problem and associated problems to the learner – continually encouraging the learner to look beyond the obvious and to really develop a thorough understanding of the problem. Once the learner develops a clear understanding of what the problem is they will probably quickly move toward appropriate ways for solving the problem.

And finally, the problem posing has to be done within an atmosphere that is built on trust between the learner and the educator. Without a strong foundation of trust between the learner and the educator the whole idea of problem posing becomes rather ridiculous and more like a game with no reason to play.

24. Change Is Constant (Every Once In Awhile)

Life is made up of alternating stages of transition and stability.

As you leave eastbound I69 at the Miller Road exit near Flint you've got to be careful because the curve comes at you pretty fast. If that isn't enough of a problem, last week as I was exiting I found myself staring at a large billboard that proclaimed, **"Change is Constant."**

What?

I got onto Miller Road and looked over my shoulder to double check. Sure enough, **"Change is Constant."** How could that be possible. The very idea of change is that it isn't constant - it's change! But wait a minute, those shrewd billboard people had done it again. They had created a way to get me to stop and reflect. And, as I reflected, I began to understand the message they were sending. They wanted me to begin to understand that I best get used to change, maybe even help change happen, because it was going to be happening to me all the time - whether I liked it or not.

Okay. They got me. Interesting way of doing it. Their message had caught me unguarded.

It took a good two more miles before it hit me. That's absurd! How could change be constant. As human beings we couldn't last. All of the research I've read clearly suggests that we proceed through life by going through alternating periods where in one period the focus is on change and in the next period the focus is on stability. We need down time following our change time. And it is through our recovery in the down time that we're able to move ahead into our next change time.

Change isn't constant. We couldn't last.

As an educator, I've always been sensitive to the idea that the best time to help adults learn was during their change time. That's the time that the adult is searching for answers to assist in the change. It's the time the adult is willing and looking for new knowledge and understandings to help him/her through the change. In fact, one of the key ideas that drives the adult during a period of change is the idea that on the other side of change will come the down time - the time of stability. It's only through a balance between change times and stable times that the adult is able to move through life with a degree of balance.

Times of change are followed by times of stability.

The adult who comes to you with a question that needs answering is most often an adult in change. Your answer can help the adult effectively accommodate the change and move on into the next period of life. And, conversely, the adult who isn't breaking down your door with questions that need answering is probably the adult who is in a stable period of life. This adult isn't needing answers at this time and for us to try to push answers onto him/her is usually rather futile.

There have been times in recent history when the teaching profession has risen to the idea that it is possible to create within the learner a time of change. It's sort of like attempting to destabilize the learner, challenging the learner with questions and dilemmas that might cause the learner to feel like he/she was in a period of transition. The rationale is that if the learner is griped by change he/she will search out learning and the teacher will be well positioned to respond. The idea of trying such a strategy with a busy adult seems to be out of the question!

As if to help me along in my thinking, this week Time magazine came out with a special issue dealing with medicine. And right at the beginning of the Introduction the editors gave me my response to the billboard:

...the process of learning, for both individuals and societies, usually comes in fits and starts.

Now that makes sense.

I've photocopied the page out of Time and have it on the visor in the car. Next week I'm heading right past Flint on the way to Port Huron and I think I'll hold it up as I go by the billboard. Maybe, though, they've changed the billboard. After all, change is constant - every once in awhile.

25. Some Days I Feel Like I'll Never Get Destinated

The need to be careful with our use of words and language.

I can't believe what we're doing to our language. Sure, I've read all of the same articles you have that go into detail on how we're destroying our language. We're reminded that bad grammar doesn't look good, slang words have their place but they shouldn't be over used and the corruption of words is often more confusing than it's worth. Well, I've had it!

It started to burn inside of me when I received a newsletter from one of our sister Big 10 institutions that described how a major program had been **"transitioned"** to them. Egad!! Then, a colleague sent me a note via email the other day that informed me he would be working on gathering information **"to feedback the committee."** Of course, there's always the group that needs to be **"inserviced."** (Every time someone tells me they're going to inservice someone I have this vivid image of a person atop a grease rack at the local service station about to be inserviced!) And, if I hear another person that's in the process of being **"orientated"** I think I'll...

Now, what's worse is that after awhile these absurdities become so commonplace that no one notices their use any more. It's almost as if a particular office or agency wants to build high walls to separate it from others. And they're doing it through their use of language. Our use of words and language can very powerfully help us fit in with our environment or set us apart from it.

As an adult educator I want to work hard to be as transparent as possible - to be a part of the community in which I work. I want to make sure my language doesn't set me apart from those I'm trying to work with.

I'm not trying to advocate against the evolution of language or the preservation of language that allows unique cultural groups to maintain their identity. What I'm trying to suggest is that we must be careful that the language we use doesn't work against the very thing that we're trying to do - establish relationships that foster learning and change. It really doesn't hurt to look at the words we use to make sure that they don't send the wrong messages to the people around us. Does our language suggest that we're trying to build walls or establish relationships? Does our language suggest that only those in the "in" really know what we're talking about? Does our language tell people that they're not smart enough to communicate with us? Does our language attempt to suggest that we're creating something new to replace something that we decided is old? Our language can speak so very loudly.

Being married to a speech and language pathologist certainly reinforces my concern. Words and their usage often find their way to the dinner table as a major focus of conversation. With a twinkle in her eye our 18 year old told her mother the other day that the difference between an electric guitar and an acoustic guitar is that one acousticates and the other one doesn't!

Okay, now I'm feeling better - I've said it. I think my message is clear.

My next challenge, though, is to figure out a new route to the Lansing Mall that doesn't take me past General Motors' Employe Development Center. Or maybe I should send this little essay to the individual at GM who thought that the word employee would be easier to spell if it ended with only one "e". Now that's absurd!!

26. On Your Mark, Get Set, Learn!

Helping the learner get off to a good learning start.

It was one of those simple ideas. Nothing at all complicated. It made so much sense once I let myself consider what was happening. It was logical. It was appropriate. It would probably significantly affect learning. Why didn't I think of it?

Before I get too far ahead of myself, let me tell you what I'm referring to.

This semester I'm teaching a new class. The focus of the class is on learning via distance education and the class participants and I have been working together to extend our understanding of this phenomena that seems to have taken higher education by storm. We have studied a variety of different delivery systems for extending education over a distance, actually experienced a number of them, become actively engaged in on-line dialogue when away from class, and entered into debates on a variety of interesting topics that surround this powerful new concept.

In other words, we are trying to learn everything we can about distance education so that we may be able to more effectively use it for teaching. However, the thing that we haven't learned to do is to understand how to help our learners understand this phenomena. We haven't discussed the sorts of fears and apprehensions that learners might have with this new technology and ways to introduce distance education to them so that they can be successful in operating within this technology. That's the simple idea that has eluded me! We need to balance our own learning of new techniques that will make us more powerful with the learning of how to introduce these techniques to learners so that they can be more powerful.

This is beginning to sound like a play within a play. Let me describe how this simple idea was introduced to me.

Last week some of us from the class met via conference call with a professor in South Carolina who has developed a new distance education course. This professor, instead of merely using distance education technology to teach his content, has created an introductory course which uses distance education technology as the focus of the course. He has decided to devote an entire course to helping the learners prepare themselves to be successful at learning at a distance.

Wow! What a great idea.

Rather than starting a class as most of us do by jumping right into our content, this professor starts by devoting an entire class to helping the learners understand what they are about to experience. And, by doing this, he is probably significantly increasing the potential for the learners to learn the content when they get to it.

It's like the overture before the opera. In the overture the composer presents all of the major themes that will be heard throughout the opera - beginning to end. This professor, in the introductory class, presents all of the key ideas that the learners are about to experience and helps them understand how they can be successful at dealing with them.

What if we as adult educators tried using such an idea? What would it look like?

Well, it might mean that we would have to start thinking differently about how we allocate our time for making a presentation or teaching a class. If we were going to make a two hour presentation we would probably want to devote the first 10 minutes to providing an overview of what we are about to do, share a handout with questions that we hope the learners might ask at the end of the presentation, identify particularly confusing topics we will be presenting, introduce the learners to any new instructional technology we will be using, and generally prepare them for our presentation. It would be just like the overture to the opera.

If we used our 10 minutes well we could expect that the learners would be ready to start at the beginning of our presentation in a learning mode. They would have warmed up during the 10 minutes and would be ready to learn what we were about to present. Questions about what we are about to do and the way in which we will be doing it would be answered. Everyone would have a good view of where we are going and how we would be traveling. We would reduce apprehension and heighten the potential for learning to occur.

On your mark, get set, learn!

27. The Plywood Approach

A strategy for temporarily unloading our "baggage"
as we quickly move to respond to a need.

My eldest daughter did an internship at a Federal agency in Washington, DC one summer. Living and working in Washington, DC was certainly an experience that contributed much to her development. And, as a proud father, I attentively listened to her stories about this and that and all of the new things she was learning.

Well, one day my ears perked up as she began a telephone conversation by saying, "Dad, I thought of you today as I had a chance to learn more about how one of our leading medical researchers approaches major tasks." Aha! The influence of the father was finally being recognized! My daughter was now linking experiences from the home with experiences of a "leading medical researcher." My mind quickly shot ahead and began thinking of all sorts of powerful lessons that might have made this trip to Washington with her.

My daughter proceeded:

"Soon after I arrived at the agency I had become aware of what was clearly the messiest office in the entire place. There were stacks of papers and books located in every available spot in the room. His desk had clearly stopped functioning as a writing surface and now joined forces with the floor as a location for more stacks of journals and articles."

Wait a minute. I was beginning to sense that my influence as a father might have just taken a wrong turn!

She continued her story:

"Everyone in my department was keenly aware of this messiest of all messy offices. In fact, you couldn't walk by the door without glancing in at the chaos and be amazed at how this researcher could possibly ever find anything."

Okay, okay. So what's the point? Certainly I hadn't agreed to pay her summer expenses just to reflect on what my office also looked like!

"Well, carefully placed behind his door and leaning up against the wall was a 4' x 8' sheet of plywood. It had been there for quite some time but the people I spoke with didn't know why it was there. All sorts of rumors had been circulated about the piece of plywood. Someone suggested that he was going to use it as kindling to start a large bonfire and rid himself of his mess. Someone else thought it was the first step in collecting building materials that would eventually be used to build an addition to his office."

"Finally one day, as I was passing the office, I caught sight of the researcher struggling with the sheet of plywood as he dragged it across the room. He positioned it alongside of his desk and then carefully lifted it high and placed it on top of the chaos of his desk. He then returned to his chair, pulled out a sheath of papers and placed them on top of this bare surface. He was now ready to work on the high priority document that must be finished by next week. And, he had an uncluttered and neat surface to use for the task."

"I had discovered what the plywood was for! Whenever he had an urgent task that needed immediate attention, he merely placed the plywood on top of the chaos for a few days to create a new surface on his desk. When finished with the urgent task he returned the plywood to its resting place ready for the next time it was needed."

"Dad, don't you have a spare piece of plywood at home?"

We both laughed. Of course, she was right. The plywood-on-top-of-the-desk strategy would probably work quite well for me. In fact, the more I thought about it the more clever this idea became.

This medical researcher had created a simple strategy that allowed him to maintain his preferred style of operating. Yet, at the same time, it allowed him to be able to quickly move to another style of operating without causing undue stress on his system! He could accommodate different demands that were placed on him in a rather ingenuous and casual way. And, he wasn't forced to clean his messy office. He probably didn't even have an ulcer problem!

What if we could approach our own work in a similar manner? How many times are we faced with situations where our own style of response doesn't seem to fit the situation? And, in how many of those situations do we dig our heels in and demand that it be done our way?

What a relief it would be if we could drag out our "plywood" and do it another way. Then, after the situation is dealt with, return the plywood to its resting place and go back to doing it "our way." The sheet of plywood metaphor could be applied to all sorts of situations where the use of an alternative approach, one that may be very contrary to how we typically operate, would move us ahead by great leaps and bounds!

28. Too Much Data And Not Enough Information

Creating a balance between data and information is the responsibility of the researcher/author.

He wasn't my student so maybe I shouldn't have been so concerned. But there he was, dragging this "monster" into my office and hefting it on to my table. I stared at it for a few seconds and then, in an attempt to buy some time, I said, "What's that?"

He proudly looked at me and proclaimed, "It's the first draft of my dissertation. It's 428 pages long!"

Of course I had known all along what it was. He had been working on his dissertation day and night for months. But I had never expected to see anything this big.

A number of thoughts immediately started racing through my mind as I tried to think of something to say. ("What could possibly be worth saying that would take 428 pages?" Or, "How in the world could anyone ever stay awake long enough to get through all of that?" Or, "Does your advisor know about this?" etc. etc.)

He was looking at me with a large smile of accomplishment - I had to say something and it better be nice! "Let's have a look," I said.

After a couple of deep breaths I opened the cover and started to glance through the document. I wasn't trying to read it, just trying to get a general impression of the thing. Aha! It seemed to read quite well. English language usage was good and I wasn't spotting any obvious typographical errors. Organization made sense and it seemed there were no major gaps in what was being presented. The writing style was consistent throughout. The charts and tables looked fine and there were lots of them. (Wow, were there ever lots of them!)

Maybe I had overreacted. Maybe this dissertation really needed 428 pages! Maybe this was one of those studies that just needed a lot of room to do it justice.

But then I got to Chapter 5 - Conclusions and Recommendations - and things became more clarified. Chapter 5 was only 15 pages long! How was it possible that a 428 page dissertation could have only 15 pages devoted to summing it all up and drawing meaning from it? It was clearly out of balance.

With my mind zeroed in on the fifth chapter I moved forward to "solve" his problem and create appropriate balance. I said, "Maybe you should try and expand the fifth chapter a bit." The student looked at me and confessed, "I've tried over and over again to enlarge the fifth chapter. I haven't had any luck doing it. I think the fifth chapter says it all. How can I make it any bigger?"

Maybe he was right. Maybe Chapter 5 wasn't the problem. Maybe the way to resolve the balance problem was to work on Chapter 4. Maybe some drastic pruning was really the answer.

And so began a touch-and-go session with the student trying his best to not be overly defensive and me trying my best to not be overly offensive. The challenge for me was clear. Would it be possible to create a balance between the data that had been collected and the amount of new information it was able to generate. Chapter 4 - the presentation of the data - had to be appropriately balanced with Chapter 5 - the meaning that was drawn from the data. There had to be a balance between data and information.

Luckily the story had a happy (and skinnier dissertation) ending. Unfortunately I've seen the same situation repeated many times when a person trying to share information from some form of research/evaluation study forgets and ends up primarily sharing data instead. There's too much data and not enough information.

This usually occurs because the author/researcher suffers from the "mountains of data" phenomena (like the student) and loses sight of the forest because of all of the trees. The data are presented according to a template in machine gun fashion. Table after table present every minuscule aspect of the study. The report looks phenomenal but the drawing of meaning is left entirely to the reader. The author/researcher stops short of drawing meaningful conclusions.

Certainly it's appropriate to allow the reader to draw his/her own meaning from a study. However, it is the responsibility of the author/researcher to also draw meaning. After all it's the author/researcher who knows the topic the best. Who better to create a balance between data and information.

29. The Perfect Job

Is a job really perfect if there aren't people
around to share your thinking with?

Trust me, I didn't provoke this one at all. I was merely sitting in my office, minding my own business, and in walks a colleague who I hadn't seen for quite awhile. Force of habit had me saying, "What's new?" before I even knew the words were out of my mouth.

The colleague, evidently needing to hear those very words of "What's new?," immediately started to update me on all of the wonderful things that were happening to him. I tried to act interested as he kept pouring them out. He whizzed past the family vacation, one child's trip to another country, the new project, and a bunch of other stuff.

Acting almost like a masochistic dentist looking to inflict pain, he worked around and around the topic until he decided it was time for the "kill" whereupon he came out with the declaration, "You know, I've got the perfect job!" I tried not to react but it was clear that he was trying to get my attention and he now had it.

I tried to act casual and uttered an "Uh-huh." He continued:

"My job is perfect. I can do whatever I want. I'm given all sorts of freedom to be creative; to initiate new projects; to look for new ideas that can help my department. No one is looking over my shoulder and pushing me in this way or that. I truly have the freedom to do whatever I think should be done. What a great job!"

I wish you could have heard his words. They weren't really very convincing. Sure, he was saying his job was perfect but it really didn't sound like it was being said by someone with a perfect job. So, I smiled and probed a bit, "Hmmm. Sounds great."

"Well, I guess the one little thing that's lacking a bit is that I really don't have anyone else in my department that's working closely with me. You know, everyone's doing their own thing, just like me. Sometimes it gets a bit hard to get excited without anyone else to share it with."

Aha, maybe the job wasn't so perfect after all! I followed with a, "Hmmm. No one to work with you," comment.

"Yeah, it makes it difficult when you don't have anyone right around you to bounce ideas off. It's such a great job, but it would be perfect if I could have a few others around me to share my thinking now and then. Don't get me wrong, though, It really is a perfect job."

Right! All of a sudden it was becoming clear that though my colleague was suggesting that his job was a perfect one it seemed that in fact it wasn't. And why? He was missing the presence of others around him that could provide opportunities for the sharing of ideas, the interaction, the sense of collegiality, the social side of learning.

After a few more minutes he was on his way. I have an idea he would be looking for others with whom he could share the sense of having the perfect job. I sat there for a while just thinking about what had just happened.

My colleague, like so many others, seemed intent on defining his perfect job in terms of the day-to-day things that he did in the job. He had freedom to move in whatever direction he felt was important. The meetings he attended would be defined according to his own blueprint. The tasks he would do grew out of what he thought was necessary. He failed to realize, though, that there was a whole other side to one's work that revolved about people and how they worked and supported what he did. And, it was the people side of his work that was clearly missing from his perfect job. In fact, the people factor might account for as much as 90% of what makes a perfect job!

How often do we fall into similar traps? We begin to see the small pieces and not the larger picture. We loose perspective as we work hard to clarify things around us. We verbalize that we're happy but our words sound very hollow and without meaning. And why?

It is often because the very obvious part of our work as an educator - the interaction with human beings - gets taken for granted and discounted. We try and give prominence to those aspects of our work that are easily countable and quantifiable in an attempt to prove to ourself and others that things are great. However, the bottom line might be just the opposite. Without people our job isn't so perfect.

So, the next time he comes around to tell me some more about his perfect job I best be ready to spend some time listening and reacting. After all, I could be one of those people that he's missing right now. And, if I and others are willing to listen and react to his ideas, his perfect job might just turn into a perfect job. All it will take is people.

30. When Life Moves To
The Default Settings

*How much of our interaction with others
is guided by us without even thinking about it?*

I was standing in line at Detroit Metropolitan Airport.
Progress was slow but at least I seemed to be inching forward toward
my goal of checking in for my flight. Finally it was my turn and I
presented myself to the agent. She smiled at me and.........**the phone
rang**.

I stood there waiting, and waiting, and waiting. I listened to
the agent talking to the other party. I tried to act casual and continued
waiting. I rocked back and forth pretending to hum a little melody in
my head. I glanced around to see how fast the other windows were
processing passengers. Finally the agent finished her conversation,
hung up the phone, checked me in for my flight and moved on to the
next customer.

It wasn't a really big thing. You see I've experienced this in
all sorts of other situations. For some reason a "higher being" has
decided that telephone calls demand immediate attention and live
people can wait.

Hmmmmm.

As I sat on the plane this thought kept replaying in my head.
Why was it that the telephone caller wasn't asked to wait for 3 or 4
minutes while the customer (*me*) who had arrived first (*me*) was
dealt with? For some reason the phone got the precedent (*not me*).
The phone was evidently the default setting (*I wasn't*)! When two
events occurred at the same time, the person in line arrived at the
same time as the ringing of the phone, the agent automatically
reverted to the default setting - answer the phone. The agent didn't

have to do a lot of thinking about the decision to answer the phone. It was easy. It was the default - answer the phone.

I stopped just short of getting very annoyed at all of this when it occurred to me that I do the same thing! And I do it all the time. Without even giving it a second thought, when the phone rings it seems to demand my immediate attention. I drop what I'm doing to answer the phone. I do it without any hint of thinking.

But how many other default settings exist in my life? How many other things do I act upon without giving them any thought? And most importantly, if I had a choice, would I keep these same default settings in my life or would I change them?

I think you can see where my mind was flowing with this one. It didn't take long to identify a variety of defaults that seemed to guide many parts of my life. However, it wasn't until I got to that last question that the "Aha" occurred. I was contemplating the "If I had a choice" question when I came to the thought, "Who said I don't have a choice?" Of course I have a choice! I just have to make sure I exercise my choice to the fullest extent.

And the parts of our life that seem to demand the greatest concern for carefully limiting the number of defaults that we have operating is the part where we interact with people. As an educator a large part of my professional life is built around interacting with people. And what a shame if a large part of my people interaction is being guided by defaults. Maybe it's time to take an inventory and decide which behaviors are operating by default in my life. Certainly they can be returned to purposeful operation rather than operating by default.

31. We Learn From Our Mistakes - NOT!

Do we really learn from our mistakes?
Or, do we learn by reflecting on our mistakes?

We've all heard it a million times. In fact, for many of us it seems that our childhood evolved around that phrase. "That's okay Joey. We can always buy a new platter. It's nothing to cry about. The next time you'll hold the platter more carefully. I think you've learned something important from this!"

Really? I can clearly remember back to those early years and the pitcher I broke, the glass of milk I spilled in my Aunt's lap as I passed it to her, and the lamp that used to be in the living room before it "accidentally" got broken. In fact, just last week I spent a few extra minutes sweeping up the remains of a casserole dish which now resides in "Broken Dish Heaven". How can it be that "we learn from our mistakes" and I'm still breaking things - still making the same mistakes? If we really learned from our mistakes wouldn't I be past this sort of thing?

As we mature into someone who is willing to take more and more responsibility for our own learning, the phrase "We Learn From Our Mistakes" seems to get new impetus as a major way of justification when we do stupid things. It's the way we rationalize the mistakes that we make. By saying that we have learned from our mistakes suggests that our mistakes weren't done in vain. After all, we have learned from them. (*Baloney!*)

Recently someone suggested to me that we learn more from our mistakes than from our successes. How does that person know? I can think of lots of times when I haven't learned from either. In the same manner in which I can make the same mistake over and over again, I've encountered times when I've searched and searched my memory to attempt to remember how to do something the right way.

I can clearly remember that the last time I had been successful with a certain task. But for the life of me I can't recall what I did that time that led me to success.

So where does this discussion take us? What difference does it make if we do or don't learn from our mistakes?

I think the key is that we have the power to learn from our mistakes. And the way we exercise this power is by taking the time to reflect. Just to make a mistake doesn't provide much learning. The learning comes about through our reflection. In other words, it isn't the mistake that we learn from - it's the reflection process that creates the learning. We learn from our mistakes if we reflect on our mistakes. If we don't reflect on our mistakes there's little chance that we'll learn from them.

I would also suggest that the phrase "Success is a powerful motivator" could similarly be tied to the idea of reflection. Success isn't much of a motivator at all until and unless we reflect on it.

On the surface the above thoughts don't seem to be very monumental. So, let's spend the last few sentences of this paper reflecting on what has been said.

Reflection #1 - **A significant role for the educator is to help the learner reflect.**

This is the way to really help learning take place. Through the process of reflection the learner begins to internalize what has happened. Through the process of reflection the learner is able to link the incident to his/her experience.

Reflection #2 - **To help the learner reflect calls for a lot of listening (to the learner) and not quite so much telling (from the teacher).**

If it's reflection that we're after, the good educator will reduce the amount of information that's delivered to the learner and focus more on reinforcing and strengthening the learner's reflection.

Reflection #3 - **Reflection works best when we're reflecting on a past action - something that we have done.**
Sometimes we get locked into a cycle and we end up reflecting on our reflections. This creates quite a lot of reflection but often doesn't lead us toward doing something better the next time.

Reflection #4 - **Reflection takes on its most powerful form when we're able to "return to the scene of the crime" and act again.**
This suggests that to really learn from a mistake takes not only some reflection but also the opportunity to try out the results of our reflection - it's the chance to try something over again without making the original mistake.

32. Feedback Or Not

Sometimes the learner misses what you are
saying and focuses on why you are saying it.

As an educator we're heavily into the business of feedback. It's the very lifeblood of our existence. Can you imagine standing in front of a group, trying your best to help them learn new ideas and concepts, with no one as much as moving a muscle to give some feedback! What a terrible situation. How would you know if anything was being learned? How would you know what questions weren't being answered? How would you even know if anyone was awake?

Of course there's also the other problem of feedback - when the feedback is *not* the type that you're looking for. Let me explain -

We had an enjoyable visit during Thanksgiving with relatives from Pittsburgh. The eldest boy is now a senior in college. (How could that be possible - yesterday he was such a little kid!). Well, it seems that Jeremy took the big leap that many students do in college - a few weeks before Thanksgiving he wrote a stinging article in the student newspaper. The expected result occurred - a landslide of *Letters to the Editor* in the week and a half following publication of the article.

I was impressed with what Jeremy had done. He had stepped outside of normal expectations and taken a lot of risk, exposing his thoughts and ideas to the reaction of others. I shared this thought with Jeremy and it was clear that he appreciated the feedback. After all, he was at a large school and the number of students these days willing to take such risks aren't too great.

Jeremy then went on to say that, though he enjoyed the notoriety, he wasn't pleased with the type of feedback that he had been receiving. It seemed that most of the letter writers (and email senders, casual conversationalists and others) were focusing their comments on his motives for writing the article rather than the actual content of the article. After all, said Jeremy, it was his ideas that he wanted to get feedback on - not the reasons why he left out certain things or included others. Why was it that so many people didn't pay much attention to **what** he had said but were unbelievably critical of **why** he had said it?

I wasn't prepared to deal with Jeremy's question since I hadn't actually seen what he had written nor the feedback he had received. However, after I returned home that evening I fired up the computer and got on the worldwide web. It took only a few minutes to find the web site for the college newspaper, Jeremy's article and the feedback that so annoyed him. After reading it through I began to understand what had happened.

Jeremy had presented a number of very powerful ideas in his article. However, his style of presentation, loaded with lots of generalizations about people and their attitudes, stood out like red flags. To the casual reader it appeared that Jeremy was standing atop a high mountain making large and encompassing statements without having much to support what he was saying. It further appeared that he had carefully omitted the use of the word "I" and took little ownership for what he was saying. No wonder the feedback he had received focused on the **why** of his article rather than the content (the **what**) of his article.

I first began to understand the difference between **what** and **why** when I had done reading in the area of moral/ethical development. Lawrence Kohlberg, a leading theorist differentiates between the **what** and the **why** of people's beliefs. He suggests that the key to understanding an individual's ethical development lies not so much in taking note of **what** they believe in but rather trying to understand **why** they believe in it. For Kohlberg the key question in response to someone making a strong statement was - **why**? (Why do you think that? Why do you feel that way? Why would you disagree with that idea? Why? Why? Why?) And, it is through an understanding of **why** that we begin to understand others around us.

So what happened with Jeremy? Well, he had not expected so much **why** feedback from his article. He had expected people to challenge the ideas that he presented and not why he had presented them. He had failed to realize that before others around him could get in touch with his ideas they needed to know the motives behind his ideas. Jeremy had expected that he could merely present his ideas as the basis for dialogue without any attention to himself - the deliverer of the ideas.

As an educator it's important to remember the **whys** behind what we're teaching. And, we should work to help our learners understand what our **whys** are. It is only after the learner begins to understand our motives that he/she can comfortably move on to consider **what** we are saying.

So, be careful in how you interpret the feedback you receive. If the learners aren't responding to the content of your message maybe they need to know some more about the motives behind why you're presenting your message. It will only take a few more minutes for you to clarify **why**.

33. Learning About Learning

*Learning a foreign language is an
interesting way to learn about learning.*

My first attempt at learning a foreign language was in high
school.[1] It had been Spanish and my teacher was a French Canadian
who had learned Spanish in the American army. What a miserable
year. I kept coming back to class, day after day, not understanding
much of anything that was being said.

My approach to trying to learn Spanish was rather
traditional. I attempted to selectively replace my English words, one
at a time, with the parallel word in Spanish. And which words would
be replaced first? The ones that the book said should be replaced
first! Learning was an exercise in remembering - remembering which
Spanish word replaced which English word. If I lived long enough I
might develop a fairly sizable vocabulary. Then one day the teacher
started talking about things like conjugation, tense, and a bunch of
other rules that had to be inserted. It now seemed that language
learning was about to become more than just a word replacement
exercise. Forget it! The language I already knew seemed to be
working quite well, thank you.

> *Maybe this is what learning is all about - a matter of
> replacing old knowledge with new knowledge. After all, it
> was what my Spanish teacher was encouraging me to do.*

My next run-in with a foreign language came a number of
years later when my wife and I vacationed in Europe. However, I
now had the perfect answer to learning a foreign language. Marry
someone who is great with languages! I didn't have to memorize a

single word. All I had to do was turn to her and say, "Dear, what did he just say?" I was set for life! Or at least I thought so.

Ah, I now have a better understanding of learning. Why do I really need to learn new information? If I ever need the information I'll just ask someone else who has previously learned it.

A visit to Tokyo a few years later provided me with the first inkling that maybe learning a language wasn't such an easy task. Not only did Japanese sound funny, but who could figure out those weird looking symbols? My colleague and I wandered about the city and talked a lot - to each other. We found a few signs in English but they didn't help a lot. Luckily most of the restaurants had those realistic looking models of their menu items attractively displayed in the front window. Our strategy for ordering was simple - we dragged the waiter out to the front window and pointed at what we wanted to eat. I can still remember the one time that we got what we had ordered!

Okay, here we are with yet another understanding of what learning is. If I'm faced with the need to know something I'll go and find a teacher who can give me the answer.

Then came the year and a half we lived in Southeast Asia. Our move had been decided in such a short period of time that learning a language before we traveled was out of the question. We'd have to learn the language as we used it. Finally I began to understand that learning another language was so much more than just substituting words in my English sentences. Learning another language was learning another way of life.

I can still remember the very first words I learned - left/kiri, right/kanan, straight ahead/terus These were survival words. Though every taxi driver assured you that he knew where he was going it was far from the truth. You spent your taxi ride sitting on the edge of the seat telling the driver what to do as he approached each intersection. "Kiri, Kanan, Kanan, Kiri, Terus…" Who would have thought these would be my first words in a new language?

Then, of course, there were the words that were never used. For instance you seldom used the word "no". Instead you got used to saying "not yet." It took a lot of the edge off of communication. Little old ladies when asked if they were married would smile and reply, "Not yet." The risk of confronting someone was eliminated. When you asked someone at the office if the report had been completed the response usually was "not yet." (It wasn't until later that I realized that I should have been asking if the report had been started! The response would have been the same, "Not yet.")

My list of Southeast Asian learnings goes on and on. Word after word. Expression after expression. All of them learned because I had a need to use them.

Hmmm. I think I've finally come to an understanding of what learning really is for me – and I think it makes a lot of sense. My learning is guided by my everyday experiences. I learn that which I have a use for.

---

[1] Of course I had learned a whole variety of Yiddish words at home when I was young. However, those words don't count since most of them can't be repeated in public!

34. Just Give Me A Second, I'll Remember What I Wanted To Say

Those inevitable educator times when you can't remember the next thing you were about to say.

I'm sure you've experienced the same sort of thing that I have when making a presentation to a group. There you are, up in front of the group, with one idea after another just popping out. It's almost like a well drilled marching band. In the same way that one band formation folds into the next, your ideas are building from one to the next. You're on a roll! The group seems to be eating out of your hand. They are not only following the ideas that you are presenting but they are also moving along with the sequence and the development of the ideas. What a great feeling. You are a naturally born educator! With a group like this and the topic that you're presenting it almost seems like you could keep going for hours. What a great feeling.

Then, it's as if a tuba player suddenly trips and the entire band loses their concentration, stops marching and just stands there doing nothing. You are building to your next point, end a sentence and realize that you don't know what you should next be saying. What are your next words? What did you just finish saying? Where am I? You immediately start talking to yourself, thereby ruining any attempt you might make to get back in step again. "I can't panic. No one yet realizes what I'm going through. I still have another few seconds to return to the topic. But what is the topic? What am I supposed to be saying?"

I can still remember so very clearly that day in Army basic training when we were all assembled out in the middle of a woods, sitting on some bleachers (*bleachers in the middle of a woods?*) listening to the sergeant teaching us about how to disassemble a rifle.

He had everything that a good teacher needed - a chalkboard, microphone and speakers, flip charts, and a long pointer. He was efficiently moving from topic to topic when all of a sudden a jet fighter plane, making an approach to the adjoining air base, nearly landed in our classroom (*at least it felt that way*). When the noise subsided we all looked at the sergeant standing there alongside the chalkboard just staring at us. It immediately became clear that the plane had also startled him and he had lost his concentration - he didn't have the vaguest idea what he was supposed to be saying. He stood there for a few very long seconds and then quickly walked behind the chalkboard, pulled out the training manual, found the page he was supposed to be on, read a few paragraphs, returned to the front of the chalkboard and continued on as if nothing had happened!

Aha! I'm not the only one with this problem. But what to do about it? Surely there are ways to help us get through such dilemmas. I suspect that we will continue to be plagued with the problem. The key is to develop a set of strategies for effectively dealing with it when it happens.

Steve Martin, writing in the **New Yorker Magazine**, discusses this very phenomena from a developmental perspective - he believes that it happens more as we grow older and move beyond the age of 50. In his article, **Changes in the Memory After Fifty**, he presents a few rather "unique" strategies for dealing with memory loss. For instance,

> "Sometimes it's fun to sit in your garden and try to remember your dog's name. Here's how: simply watch the dog's ears while calling out pet names at random. This is a great combination with 'Name That Wife' and 'Who Am I?'"

Or, another of Martin's compensating strategies for memory loss relates to the idea that the brain is full - it simply has too much data to compute:

> "This is easy to understand if we realize that the name of your third-grade teacher is still occupying space, not to mention the lyrics to 'Volare.' One solution for older men is to take all the superfluous data swirling around in the brain and download it into the newly large stomach, where there is plenty of room. This frees the brain to house more relevant information, like the particularly troublesome 'days of the week.'"

So where does this leave us? How, in fact, can an educator like me deal with the inevitable "Where am I?" phenomena that appears periodically. Here are a few ideas:

- Try not to get into a situation where you talk for long stretches of time. Look for ways to break up these long stretches so you have some of your own thinking/organizing time for your own ideas. Probably the easiest way to do this is to periodically encourage comments and reactions from your group of learners.
- Avoid using a script as the way to help your memory. Chances are it will sound like you're reading a script (*you are!*). In addition the group will probably go in directions that your script doesn't permit.
- Have a sheet of paper ready and available for taking notes. Get in the habit of taking notes on things that you see and hear during your program. Use the sheet to help jog your memory when necessary about things that you want to make sure you cover. Whenever you stumble upon a "Where am

I?" situation, glance at your sheet of paper to get some quick ideas to continue your presentation.

- Organize your presentation ahead of time. Take time to prepare an outline that includes the key ideas and concepts that you'll be covering. Keep the outline in front of you so you can always see where you are.

There was another idea that I wanted to include here, but for the life of me I can't remember what it was.

35. Customer Or Learner?

Do we sell ourselves short by adopting a
consumer view of our role as educator?

More and more we're hearing about the customer or the consumer as the person who must be the focus of our attention as an adult educator. The student or learner has been pushed aside and replaced with this new consumer image. Starting in the world of commercialism, the customer has now been moved to a central position in so much of what we do. I was startled recently when this idea was elevated to new heights. It came to me in a newsletter from the largest adult education system in the United States – the Cooperative Extension Service.

"The most successful Cooperative Extension System units are meeting clients' needs so well that the prized consumers return again and again. Repeat business and acclaim tell us we are doing things right and exceeding client expectations! We share with corporate America the commonality of the best methods to promote products and support consumer retention activities. There are great opportunities for Extension professionals to apply proven customer retention techniques used by the best business corporations."

I couldn't believe what I had just read. It didn't sound like education at all. There was no sense of relationship with a human being. It sounded like the writer was describing an approach that should be used by my local hardware store!

But as I reflected for a few minutes I realized it didn't sound like my local hardware store at all. Absolutely not. I enjoy going to my local hardware store because I'm *not* treated as a customer - I'm treated as a friend who has a problem. And because of this my hardware store has a revered place on my list of local learning resources. If Ray is busy when I arrive at my hardware store (*Ray knows everything there is to know about house construction*), Walt will help me think through what I need. Sure, I buy things at the hardware store. However, I leave with so much more than just a purchase.

I leave the hardware store with new ideas. I leave with an answer to the problem that I arrived with. And better yet, I often leave with my problem reconceptualized thanks to the help of Ray and Walt and the others. And most importantly, I leave with a sense that I can now solve the problem that I came in with.

I think this is what education is all about - having the learner leave with new ideas, answers to problems, new insights of what the problem really is, and a sense that he/she can solve the problem that is being faced. It's certainly not about selling something to a customer.

So, is it a hardware store or is it a learning laboratory? Hmmmm. Maybe it's both!

> *They announced last week that construction will soon begin locally on one of those large mega-stores that sells all sorts of hardware and building materials. It will be about a mile from the hardware store. When it opens I'm sure there will be considerable advertising and other forms of marketing to attempt to lure customers from every direction. Clearly they will be attempting many things so the "prized consumers return again and again." They'll be spending big bucks to "promote products and support consumer retention".*

So, how will the fellows at my hardware store be able to compete with such tremendous buying/advertising power. Easy! They'll just keep doing what they have been doing. They will continue treating people that walk through the door as people - people who have turned to them for answers. And, as good neighbors, they will listen well and share ideas. Dialogue will continue to replace salesmanship. The door will remain open for people to return in the future. And when they're not busy trying to help someone, they'll be scouring their numerous sources for new ideas and devices. After all, they're in business to help me - whether they happen to be a local hardware store clerk or an extension educator.

36. Visualizing Learning

Julius Nyerere's idea of how to help people learn.

Julius Nyerere, the former President of the African nation of Tanzania, was a rather remarkable individual. President of Tanzania from 1961 to 1985, Nyerere devoted much of his time to defining African solutions to Africa's problems. And, rather uniquely, was one of the very few African leaders who, after leaving office, was able to stay and work in his own country. He had no fear of the people he had served because he worked hard to serve them.

My purpose in mentioning Julius Nyerere, however, relates to another aspect of him. It was his nickname. He was called "*Mwalimu*," the Swahili word for "teacher." When all was said and done, Nyerere saw himself, more than anything else, as a teacher. It's a title he was proud of and had been the basis of some of his best writing.

I remember reading an essay by Nyerere that he used for an examination of the whole idea of educational program planning. It seemed he had done his homework. He described the very steps that most of us pride ourselves in following when it comes to creating a scheme whereby people can change their lives through learning. He discussed the need for participation with the learners, the identification of learning needs, the setting of appropriate goals and objectives, the defining of viable teaching strategies, and even threw in some ideas about evaluating success and feeding the results back into the design so that it might be improved the next time. It all made sense. It was the way we were supposed to do it.

I stopped congratulating myself, however, when I got to the paragraph where Nyerere suggested that *these were all wonderful steps but they would never work!!*

Wait a minute. Every textbook on educational program planning/ implementation mentioned these steps. How could he be so presumptuous to suggest that they were wrong and would not work. Certainly he must have been naive. Maybe I had stumbled upon a major error in the powerful thinking of *Mwalimu*. I quickly moved on to find out why he thought that the standard educational program approach was insufficient. And, there it was in the next paragraph - *if the learner was not able to **visualize** himself/herself as having achieved the goal then there was little possibility that the learner would actually achieve the goal.* We had to invest our energies in helping the learner develop a visualization of having achieved the goal. Then, and only then, was it useful to continue on with the normal steps of the educational program.

At first it seemed to be just a jumble of words. I repeated the idea over in my mind a few times. Nyerere was saying that the very first step in working with a learner was to help the learner develop a visual image. And, the visual image was of the learner having triumphed and achieved the very goal of the learning plan. It was starting to make some sense - at least I was understanding the point he was trying to make.

Nyerere was suggesting that the real key to success in learning was the motivation of the learner. Somehow you had to work to enlist the motivation of the learner at the beginning of teaching to insure success. And the way to enlist the motivation of the learner was to help the learner begin the process by viewing himself/herself as being successful. If the learner had such a visual image then it was only a matter of working to make the image become real. And, conversely, if the learner had no image of himself/herself achieving the learning goals then the learner wasn't much of a help - the teacher had to try and do it all!

The fog finally cleared when I began to personalize Nyerere's message. I remembered the many times that I had attempted to stop smoking. It seemed to never work. I was off cigarettes for a few weeks and then back on again. I knew I wanted to stop smoking but it never seemed to last - until I tried the last time. And that time it worked.

I visualized myself as a non-smoker. I played through different scenarios in my mind where I was offered a cigarette. Each time I would respond with the statement, "No thank you. I don't smoke." I liked the image of myself as a non-smoker and then it became so much easier. I worked to fulfill the image of myself as a non-smoker.

Nyerere's idea of helping the learner visualize "success" as the beginning step of learning is such a powerful idea. When I think of the times that I'm most successful as an educator they tend to be the times when the learners have a clear visualization of themselves as having succeeded. They look to me for specific help in fulfilling the image they have of themselves. It's the reason why the graduate student who had dropped out of sight so long ago can return and finish the degree in no time at all. It's the reason why one person at a workshop seems to find the information so meaningful and is ready to put it to use yet another person thinks the program is a waste of time.

Now that I understand Nyerere's message I've been working on being able to visualize myself in the role of helping others in the visualizing process. It's sort of like a play within a play. I think it's going to help me become a more powerful educator!

37. You Should Live So Long

When learning doesn't occur at
the same time as the teaching.

I was reminded the other day of an old-time vaudeville comedian that had been a fixture on Baltimore's notorious East Baltimore Street at the Gayety Burlesque (long since closed). I can't begin to think of his name but I still remember his typical retort to just about any sort of on-stage comment. Without even thinking, he'd come out with, "You should live so long!" It was delivered with a deadpan look and usually came in response to anyone suggesting something that seemed to be good in some way for them.

"I think this is going to be my lucky day at the race track!"
"You should live so long."
"Can I borrow ten bucks?"
"You should live so long."
"Wouldn't it be great to own a new car!"
"You should live so long."

I think you get the picture. The vaudeville comedian would issue his response to just about anything that was said - especially something that had a positive intention.

So why on earth would I be remembering such trivia? Well, my thoughts had been triggered when I recently bumped into a person who had attended a workshop I had presented 4 years ago on the topic of personal and professional development. At that time I had presented the eight developmental stages of Erik Erikson and tried to help the group understand how they might have more control of their personal and professional life if they understood Erikson's theory - especially the stages yet to be encountered.

The group was polite, actively participated in the activities that I had designed, and asked what appeared to be good questions. As I looked around the room it was clear that about half of the group were really in tune with what I was saying.

The other half, in response to my attempts to help them learn, seemed to be saying, "You should live so long!"

Well, guess what? The person I had bumped into the other day had been in the "You should live so long" group. She had been content with her own answers to the ideas that I had presented. She was courteous but clearly not in any mood to have her thinking challenged. Her ideas had worked for many years - why should she change. When it came to new ideas her response was clearly, "You should live so long."

But something had changed! Her greeting to me the other day was one of excitement. She couldn't wait to share her thoughts with me about that old program she had attended. As she recounted the ideas from that old program it was as if it had happened just yesterday. She described each of the main ideas and how much each of them now really made sense to her.

I, of course, listened and said the right sorts of things to reinforce what clearly had turned into some significant learning for her. When the right time came I casually inserted the question I really wanted to ask, "Why has this information now become important to you when it wasn't so important four years ago?"

Her answer was certainly predictable. Her life had changed significantly in these four years. And, the ideas from the old program now made sense in terms of the things she had recently been experiencing. She was now ready to learn these things. She hadn't been ready four years ago.

Aha - it had finally happened. The old vaudeville comedian was wrong. **I had lived so long**!! I had arrived. I had achieved the very thing that the old vaudeville comedian felt sure would never happen. If he only knew!

As I reflected I began to wonder if there had been something that I could have done to insure that I would "live so long." Here's what I came up with:

- Getting better at listening to learners can really help. Rather than trying to only push my ideas I should work on hearing their concerns and then linking my ideas to theirs. Of course, this gets harder and harder as the size of the group gets larger and larger (maybe I should try and limit the number of people attending a program - this could improve my chances of listening to the learners).
- Creating participatory learning activities that can be used during the program can help the learners "tell me" what they want to learn. It's not sufficient to merely say, "What do you want to learn?" Learners will usually speak very loudly through their actions - if we create good opportunities for the learners to demonstrate their actions.
- Developing a clear idea, before the program, of what the learners may want to know. This is especially important if I'll only be seeing the learners on a single occasion. And, of course, making sure I design the program so that it can be changed if my ideas of what they want to know aren't correct.

It's okay not to always have the feeling that learning has occurred at the very same time that we have presented the ideas. Realistically, there's never any guarantee that learning will occur on such a schedule. And, sometimes it occurs years after a program has been presented. It would be nice if learning occurred right along with the teaching but it is certainly not a realistic expectation. It's okay if it's delayed. The big thing is that it actually does occur at some time. And, if you do it right, "You will live so long!"

38. What Do You Mean They Aren't The Enemy?

Moving the classroom lectern so everyone fits on the same side.

"You heard me right. They aren't the enemy. It's really absurd to consider them as the enemy."

"But every time I get up in front of a group of people at a program that I'm presenting I have this feeling that the audience is about to get me. You know, it's as if they are getting ready to shoot me down - as if they are the enemy."

"I can understand your feelings, but you've got to get it out of your head - they aren't the enemy."

"Okay Mr. Big shot. You say you understand my feelings. So tell me, why do I feel this way? Why do I perceive them as the enemy?"

"I think your feelings began with your early schooling experiences - experiences where it seemed that school was very adversarial. It was sort of a 'me versus they' phenomena. Often the situation existed whereby neither the students nor the teachers wanted to be there and they were always blaming the other for their imprisonment. Learning in such a situation was like a battlefield with only one 'winner' allowed. And, the winner was often the 'tall one' who stood at the front of the room lecturing at us 'little ones.' Now I realize that wasn't always the case, but you dared not let your guard down for too long a period of time. If you did, the dreaded win-lose scenario would appear and before you knew it you would have lost another battle."

"Hmmmm"

"This adversarial baggage often follows us right into the teaching/learning setting with adults as learners. Without even thinking about it we automatically assume that those people on the other side of the lectern are the enemy - our adversaries. Sometimes we bring it on all by ourselves. At other times the adult learners push us into a corner taunting us into an adversarial battle.

> *"Absolutely! Just last week I did a presentation to a local group and about half way through I found myself fighting for my life. It seemed that everything I said was being challenged by someone in the audience. I couldn't say or do anything right! What should I have done to see the learners in a different light? Could I have reduced the adversarial relationship?"*

"I think the way to begin is to move the lectern! I don't mean this literally - just figuratively. In other words, move the lectern far enough to allow everyone - you and the learners - to be on the same side of it. The lectern often serves as a clear indication of where the line has been drawn for the battle. We don't need such a line when we're helping adults learn."

> *"Okay, so I'll move the lectern. But then the group will clearly see how my knees are shaking when I'm up in front! That's going to be embarrassing for me."*

"It's okay to have shaky knees - especially if the shaking comes from you trying to do a good job. I have developed a small list of my own strategies for getting rid of shaky knees. Sometimes I'm successful. Sometimes I'm not. But it's always worth a try. Here's my list:"

- "First, I make sure I'm prepared. Not only do I review the content that I'll be presenting but I also carefully review my schedule of what happens first, second, and third. I find that the better prepared I am the more flexible I can be. That sounds like a contradiction but it really works. If I'm well prepared I can afford to veer from my schedule. If I'm not well prepared I stick to my schedule for security. If I'm well prepared I can hear what the learners are really asking. If I'm not well prepared I'm too busy trying to remember what I'm supposed to be saying and never relax enough to hear the learners - their questions, their concerns, their comments."
- "Second, I try to practice a bit of reciprocity. Since I want the learners to learn from me I make sure I also learn from them. In other words, I work to create a reciprocal learning relationship. There's nothing quite so powerful (and reassuring) for the learners then to sense that the teacher is also learning at the session. It creates a learning "community" with all of us in the same boat."
- "And third, I work to make sure I don't use too many quick answers. True, I'm there to help provide answers, but I have to learn to slow down and not throw out my answers too quickly. By slowing down I improve my chances of truly hearing what's on the mind of the learners. This also creates a situation where other learners have the opportunity to add their own answers to the question. I find that once the interaction begins to open up (and it's not just me trying to answer each question) my shaky knees subside a tremendous amount."

"That's my small list!"

"Whoa - that sounds too easy! I was expecting a bit more of a theoretical basis for moving the lectern. Do you mean to say that by using these few techniques I'll be able to back away from seeing the learners as the enemy?"

"Well, I think you're rushing to a conclusion. It's certainly not just a matter of a few techniques. Techniques are a beginning. However, when you are truly able to stand on the same side of the lectern as the learners, interacting with them as co-learners and co-teachers, you will no longer be in an adversarial relationship - something that usually works against helping people learn."

"It sounds like what you're trying to do to help people learn is to engage them in a conversation. Sort of like the one we're having right here on this paper."

"Hmmmm"

39. Directions For Reading This Book

Wouldn't it be great if we could issue instructions
to our learners and require they follow them. Or would it?

Somewhere along life's journey I got caught up with the
writing of Philip Wylie. Wylie was a rather prolific writer from the
1920's into the 1950's. Among his more memorable works were
Gladiator (the eventual model for Superman), **When World's
Collide** (made into what is considered the first really classic science
fiction movie), **Tomorrow, Triumph, An Essay on Morals, Opus
21, The Answer** and a host of other fiction and non-fiction works.
(Wylie even managed to write a regular series of fiction for the
Saturday Evening Post dealing with the exploits of two charter boat
fisherman - Crunch & Des.)

Recently I happened upon an original edition of **Generation
of Vipers** - a searing essay dealing with what Wylie viewed as the
complacency of Americans. Written in less than two months in 1942,
Vipers managed to startle just about everyone in one way or another.
In fact, twelve years after it's publication, Wylie wrote that he had
heard from fifty or sixty thousand people!

As I began skimming through my latest copy of **Vipers** I
noticed that it was different. The numerous footnotes I was familiar
with had evidently been written for later editions and weren't
included in this first one. And, of course, the "Introduction" that was
found in all of the revised editions wasn't there either. What peaked
my interest was a short section at the very beginning of the book that
had also been eliminated in later editions. This short section was
entitled, "*Directions for Reading This Book*."

Yup - sounds just like Philip Wylie! Never one to miss an
opportunity to challenge the reader. And this time he wasn't taking
anything for granted. He was going to sit right down with you and

give you a few pointers on getting the most out of his writing. So what *Directions* did Wylie have for the reader?

First, he stated that the book "must not be read at a single sitting." He compared his writing to a bottle of brandy and suggested that it would be impossible to "master the whole of it at a gulp." He went on to suggest that it wasn't necessary to read the book from beginning to end. It could be "started anywhere and even read backwards, chapter by chapter. For pure adventure, commencement anywhere is suggested."

Wylie was concerned that the reader understand what the book "was" and not get overly focused on what it "wasn't." He sensed that readers might see his book to be "one vast gripe" and suggested that if that was the case they "had better read the book again."

Finally, Wylie let it all out in the concluding paragraph of his *Directions*:

> "Minors should not read this book. Neither should lip-movers and finger-pointers. If you enjoy this book, I would be glad if you wrote and told me so; I would be gladder still if you wrote the editors of your favorite magazines and asked them why they did not hire me to write like this. And if you do not enjoy this book, the devil take you!"

As I sat digesting Wylie's instructions I was challenged to think through what I might do with my own teaching if I were to include a set of *Directions* for the learners. What things would I say to make sure they would learn the important things that I would be saying?

I started with the notion that I'd like my learners to hear what I was saying and not just to take notes. (Maybe my *Directions* would outlaw pencils in my class!) And, how would they know if they were really hearing me? Well, I guess I'd ask that they try to act on what they were hearing - do something with the information. That would be a great way for them to see if they had heard it right.

Next I'd instruct them to ask questions and challenge the ideas that are presented. There's no greater way for an instructor to feel at ease than to have a group of learners who are comfortable enough to speak up. Of course I'd have to demand that they keep their questioning and challenging in a positive vain. And, if they weren't able to be positive they should be quiet, not asking any questions, and sit through the class another time!! (Thanks, Mr. Wylie!)

I'd probably want to direct the learners to look around themselves for answers – not to be dependent on me to deliver all of the answers to them. I'd provide a listing of all of those other learning resources that they would have to work at learning from - classmates, friends, family, etc. My *Directions* would, like Wylie's, demand that the learners not try to learn it all in one class - let it take some time to settle in and be put into practice.

I think I'm on a roll! I could specify lots and lots of things that I would expect the learners to accommodate if they wanted to "learn from my class."

Oops - wait a minute!

*Suddenly, as if being awoken from a dream, I had this vision of my learners, getting out of their seats as a group and walking to the front of my classroom. (I don't remember my **Directions** telling them they could do this.) One of the learners stepped to the front of the group and handed me a folder. As I began to open the folder my worst fear was confirmed. There, written clearly across the top of the first sheet of paper it said, **Directions for Teaching This Class**.*

40. Picture This –

*Using a more "open" teaching style to allow the
learners to build themselves into the picture.*

I'm never quite sure what to expect when I receive a present
from my youngest daughter. She's been known to lay awake nights
plotting elaborate schemes of what to buy and when to present them
to me (there's nothing to compare to a Sunday family dinner with me
opening an elaborately wrapped gift of underwear from my
daughter!).

Recently she demonstrated that she hasn't lost her touch. A
package came in the mail. I knew who it was from. And I suspected
she was up to no good once again.

I opened it slowly, not sure of exactly what I would find. It
was flat, about the size of a school notebook. Inside I found a note,
"Dad, I immediately thought of you when I saw this. I had to buy it
for you!"

I was in trouble!

Inside was a frameable print. It was an old-time photograph
showing the front of a Paris train station. You know the type of
station - massively constructed out of stone that looks like it will
stand for thousands of years. Well, propped up against the outside
wall of the railroad station is a very large steam engine that has just
punched through the second story and come to rest with the nose
lodged in the street and the back of the engine resting against the
building. I'm sure you can picture it - this massive monument of a
building with the absurdity of a steam engine having crashed through
the wall - sort of helplessly dangling from the second story.

She was right. It was my kind of picture. It not only played
on my fascination with railroads but it also included a sense of
absurdity - something she knows I enjoy.

137

The picture did not include any caption or title. I really had no idea what the person who decided to publish the picture had in mind. So, as I studied the picture all sorts of phrases and thoughts started to run through my head. "*I told you to check the brakes before we left Marseilles!*" Or, "*Who stole the 'End of Track' sign?*" Or, how about, "*Does this mean I won't be getting my engineer's license?*"

As I continued to study the photograph I knew that the only place to hang it would have to be in my office. Why waste the power of this image at home where I would probably be the only one to notice it. At the office it would be seen by a number of people, many of whom could no doubt "benefit" from its message. It could certainly be helpful in stimulating graduate students to continue their journey on the way toward a graduate degree. I could imagine a variety of reactions to the photograph when seen through the eyes of a graduate student. It could evoke images (hopefully in a tongue-in-cheek fashion) of where the chaos of graduate school seemed to be heading for so many students - like an out of control railroad engine crashing through the terminal wall. It could suggest that even the best constructed plans can often go astray. It would certainly bring an immediate smile to even those who tend to be way too serious most of the time.

This was fun - thinking of some of the many possible messages that the photo could evoke. It was as if the photograph had been created especially for me and my imagination. How did my daughter manage to get a present for me that was so powerful that it easily allowed me to build myself into it? Did she know where my mind was going to take the photograph?

As I continued to generate possible new meanings that could be derived from the photograph I became increasingly aware of the parallel between what was occurring with me and what often happens in our world of teaching. As a teacher I sometimes provide a "present" to the learners which allows them to creatively draw their

138

own meanings - to build themselves into it. The learners don't seem to be upset that the "present" does not outwardly relate to the specified learning objectives for the session. They seem to be able to take the "present", and in their own way, have it generate meaningful and relevant learning for themselves. Of course this appears to be contrary to what we have been taught. We have been taught to carefully select that which we present in our teaching to make sure that it relates very directly to the instructional objectives for the session. However, is it okay if we use an idea, concept or "answer" as part of our teaching if it doesn't clearly respond to a specific instructional objective for our session? Absolutely! Obviously it can't be done all of the time because that could become very confusing for the learners. They would begin to wonder where any of the instruction is leading.

However, it is very acceptable to periodically include such open-ended components in our teaching. And why?

We can't be so presumptuous to always assume we know what it is that the learners want to learn from us or, in fact, will learn from us. By allowing the learners the freedom to build themselves into the instruction they may be better able to draw meaning from what we have presented. We must be able, at times, to trust the learners to draw their own important meanings from our teaching - meanings that we may have never considered.

Think back to the photograph my daughter gave me. What if she only gave me presents which perfectly fit my needs and moved me only in the direction I had previously specified to her? How boring! Of course, I don't think I'll ever have that problem with her. (It's also nice to know that my other daughter spends hours and hours trying to figure out exactly the right present to fit my needs!)

41. Relaxing And Learning

Trying to alter the relaxation-learning continuum.

There seems to be a fine point in what I fondly refer to as the "relaxation-learning continuum" when there is a perfect balance between how relaxed I feel and how much I'm able to learn. I'm sure you've experienced the same phenomena. In fact, I suspect that we each have a balance point that is unique to our own relaxation-learning continuum.

Here's what I mean –

I come home from a busy day at work, have supper and then sit down to read the newspaper. Within minutes I'm sound asleep.

Ooops - I didn't hit the balance point! Clearly I was too far over on the relaxation end of the continuum and not far enough on the learning end. And the result is a great nap with zero learning.

Okay, here's the same scenario with a different twist –

I come home from a busy day at work, have supper and then sit down to read the newspaper. I sit there for awhile staring at the newspaper but nothing is sinking in. I make it through the headline okay but I've been rereading the same article for 10 minutes with absolutely no comprehension. Then I realize that I've been replaying in my mind a problem I had faced earlier in the day - still searching for the answer.

Again I've missed the balance point but this time it seems that I'm too far over on the learning end of the continuum so I'm not able to relax. I end up doing some learning but I risk getting a stiff neck as I do it.

I'm sure you have your own set of examples of when you've been at one or the other end of the continuum. And, examples of when you've hit it right on the head with learning and relaxation being perfectly in balance.

Now for a sobering thought. The next time you're involved in teaching a class of some sort, look around the room and try to understand where each person is in terms of their own personal relaxation-learning continuum. It won't take much practice before you get real good at deciding where people are. Then the challenge is to try and alter the situation! Try to create a teaching/learning situation where people are appropriately balanced between relaxation and learning.

At the beginning of this past semester I tried out this idea of looking around the room to get a sense of where the 10 learners in my seminar were on the relaxation-learning continuum. No surprise! It was a graduate seminar and as could be expected they were all leaning heavily toward the learning end of the continuum. Now don't get me wrong, it's not bad to have your audience on the learning end of the continuum. However, it would be great if it were possible to have the learners at the perfect balance point between relaxation and learning. If that were possible it would probably make for a very enjoyable teaching/learning experience for all of us.

So, I decided to try something a bit different! After the first few weeks of the seminar I invited everyone to continue our meetings at my home. We then spent the remaining 10 weeks of the semester meeting each Tuesday afternoon for 3 hours in my family room. I set up a flipchart to be used when needed, we had easy access to the VCR, plus there were refreshments available for each session. Clearly the relaxation side of the continuum had been brought more clearly into focus. And the results were remarkable!

Discussions became much more lively, people listened more intently, and everyone seemed to arrive each week more willing to accept responsibility for the success of our session. The potential for learning seemed to increase significantly as the opportunity to be comfortable and relax was added to the formula. In fact, it was interesting to note that the usual mid-session break - something that had always been essential as a part of classroom instruction - disappeared from our sessions. We went for the entire three hours without a formal break. People who needed a quick break could do it on their own with no need to disrupt the others in the group. And, no one seemed to miss the break.

Altering the "classroom" to better accommodate the relaxation side of the continuum seemed to bring everyone in the seminar much closer to a viable balance point. And when that happened the entire atmosphere shifted. It was fun to teach and learn!

(P.S. I just checked the enrollment for the seminar I'll be teaching in the upcoming semester. I've got 16 students enrolled! There's no way I'll be able to fit that many in our family room. Will I have to move back toward the learning end of the continuum? Or, will I be able to find another strategy for allowing my learners to relax and find their balance point? Hmmmmm.)

42. Please Move To The Rear Of The Elevator

Wouldn't it be nice if life went
as smoothly as an elevator?

I think I had an **Aha!** today. I'm sure you know what I mean. It happens when you find yourself in a situation and you suddenly gain clarity into something that you didn't even know was bothering you. It's almost like a bright spotlight is turned on for just a second and it illuminates something in your life. You find yourself almost audibly saying **Aha!**

My **Aha!** happened as a function of riding the elevator up to my office. It was a subtle **Aha!** and I almost missed it. The elevator got to my floor, the doors opened, and I stood there staring at the hallway. It only took a second or two but there I stood. No one else was on the elevator and no one was waiting to board. After a second or two the doors closed and there I was, still standing idly in the elevator. No movement. The elevator just stayed there with me inside. Really quiet. It was as if I was waiting for something to happen.

Suddenly I awoke from my stupor, pushed the button, the doors opened and I exited on my floor.

Now for the **Aha!**. You see, the **Aha!** didn't hit me in the elevator. The **Aha!** came to me as I sat at my desk trying to make some sense out of what had just happened. I replayed the scene in my mind as if it was a videotape. There I was, standing in the elevator like a fool, staring blankly out as the doors opened and closed with me on the inside. Why didn't I get off when the doors opened?

I knew the basic answer to my question. The basic answer was that I was obviously deep in thought contemplating something or other. However, I wanted to get at the underlying answer, the *real* answer. "So, Joe, what were you *really* thinking about?"

As the fuzz started to clear I remembered back years ago to a colleague who had gotten stuck in an elevator due to a malfunction of the mechanism. He had spent almost two hours stuck in the elevator before the local fire department was able to "rescue" him. When he was finally rescued he merely thanked everyone, walked away and went about his business. There was no major speech describing how scarred he was, how the eminent danger of the situation had gripped him, how he had hollered for help, etc.

Later that day I caught up with him and asked him what had happened. His comment was, "Evidently something had gone wrong with the elevator." I, of course, responded with, "Well, what did you do?" His reply was, "Nothing." "Nothing? What do you mean you did nothing? Didn't you at least ring the emergency bell?" He told me he hadn't thought of ringing the emergency bell. In fact the first thing that had crossed his mind was that there was no phone in the elevator for people to bother him. Second, he had a whole briefcase full of paperwork that needed his attention. And third, what a great, quiet place to work! So, he sat down on the floor of the elevator and proceeded to go about his work. Evidently the "rescue" occurred when others became concerned. It wasn't his initiative that got the fire department to help him!

My **Aha!** came to me at the same time I remembered this story of my colleague. I suddenly realized that my immobility in the elevator was not an accident. It wasn't, as I had first assumed, a minor slip in my attention span. No, it was (**Aha!**) because I didn't want to get off the elevator! How simple an answer.

My mind now jumped around with this realization. I quickly conjured up a great "elevator metaphor" with everyone uncontrollably pushing the buttons and demanding to be taken to their floor. Of course, everyone was in a hurry and wanting to go to their floor first. People were annoyed when the elevator stopped at all of the floors - especially if there was no one entering or exiting. Sometimes the door closed slowly and people got upset because they were wasting time. At other times people got cut off by the door as it closed too quickly thereby causing them to thrust their hand into the narrowing opening trying to halt the progress of the elevator so that their need to exit could be accommodated.

So there it was, a message disguised as an elevator. Most interesting.

Clearly the elevator served as both a symbol of a quiet refuge for me (no wonder I didn't want to get off) and also a symbol of lots of people making lots of demands. Hmmmm. An interesting dual picture. How is it possible for one thing to be both peaceful and demanding? I guess that's really what life is all about - trying to accommodate the opportunity to have a sense of quiet refuge while, at the same time, knowing that there are people surrounding you that keep pushing your buttons.

Now if only life would be more like the elevator - quietly and reliably responding to the constant demands of people. Able to sort out lots of conflicting commands and still maintaining a certain peacefulness. Wouldn't that be great. Or would it? Come to think of it, the elevator does well because it never leaves that narrow elevator shaft. How boring! I guess I'll just have to get better at dealing with life as it comes.

P.S. If you see me on an elevator, riding for a seemingly long period of time - just ignore me. I'll be getting off when I'm ready.

43. Turning A Pet Peeve Into A Generalizable Concern

*The challenge of feeling responsible
for helping the learner learn.*

We all have our own pet peeves. Sometimes they are very large. Usually they are rather small. Typically we don't broadcast them to others since they usually relate to our own uniqueness and others just wouldn't understand. We do, however, tend to share them with those who are close to us, hoping that we will gain the reassurance that a particular pet peeve is really worthy of the world's attention. (*My wife has begun to realize that watching the evening news with me can turn into a most disturbing event as I pick apart the behavior of our local newscasters. It seems that I have a whole bunch of pet peeves that relate to the art of newscasting!*)

The reason why pet peeves don't deserve a wide audience is that they usually don't generalize to anything else. They are unique to us, annoy us tremendously, but really don't have much to say to others.

Once in awhile we are able to elevate a pet peeve to a message that we feel others have a real need to know. This happens when we find some sort of message within our pet peeve that is worth sharing. I think I found one of these.

It started out as a very typical "*fast food restaurant pet peeve.*" How many times have you watched your order at a fast food restaurant get turned upside down as it gets passed from one person to another in the process of being fulfilled. Here's what happens. You place your order with one person whose real responsibility is only collecting your money. This person usually pretends to be interested in your order. Somehow, during the process of collecting your money, your order is magically telegraphed to another person who is responsible for packaging your order. This person, in turn, announces your order to a variety of people - a cook who is suffering from short term memory problems, a person operating a deep fryer who just broke up with his girlfriend, and a "free agent" who is wandering amidst the commotion of the others in an attempt to find more ketchup packets. At some point your order gets flopped into a paper bag, placed into your hands, and the packager - already dealing with the next person in line - manages to mumble a "**Have a good day**" in your general direction.

And, as I'm sure you've experienced it, your order turns out to be only a faint resemblance of what you had originally paid for. It seems that no one has any sense of responsibility toward you or your order. It is a very specialized situation with no one taking responsibility to see that you get what you had planned on. And, when it breaks down (as it often does) there seems to be no one who feels responsible to make corrections. Maybe my "*fast food restaurant pet peeve*" is really an "*Egad, why do we need so much specialization around us pet peeve.*"

I'll never forget the time I broke a tooth at a restaurant. As I approached the cashier's counter I was greeted with, "How was everything?" I thought twice about mentioning my misfortune but decided it was worthy of sharing. I commented, "The food was fine but I broke my tooth." Without even looking at me the cashier continued counting out my change, deposited it in my hand, and uttered the ubiquitous, "Have a nice day." Evidently she wasn't empowered in her job to listen to the customer, only to make change and utter her "Have a nice day" phrase. Too much specialization!

A recent encounter that my wife had with the medical community immediately reminded me of the same pet peeve. It was as if she had mistakenly arrived at a fast food restaurant rather than a medical laboratory. After being questioned about the purpose of her visit by three different laboratory staff - one after another - she was greeted finally by the person who was responsible for actually running the test. And, you guessed it, the first thing that this person said was, "Exactly why are you here?" Whoa - what happened to all of the testimony that my wife had just provided to the other practitioners? What did these other people do with the information? If they didn't need the information, why did they ask for it? Were the three other staff members there just to provide a rehearsal opportunity for my wife. I don't think so! They were suffering from too much specialization. No one seemed to be seeing the big picture.

Aha! That was it - seeing the big picture. My pet peeve was now into the generalization stage. It was no longer just a figment of my own annoyance but was now ready to be considered in relation to a bigger message with relevance to other things!

What happens in our society when people lose sight of the bigger picture and don't feel a sense of responsibility toward the person? Now that is a lot more than merely a pet peeve. That's a real concern. It's generalizable to many situations - especially situations where we as educators may fall into the same trap.

As an educator we must be able to maintain a strong sense of responsibility to the learner. We can't go asking them for information, over and over again, and not use the information we receive. We can't allow ourselves to fall back into being a non-responsible person as if we were working on an assembly line (or a fast food restaurant, or a medical laboratory). The way we exercise our responsibility toward the learner is by being able to continually step back from the teaching/learning situation and see that what we are doing relates to the life and concerns of the learner. We have to be careful to not get caught up in a specialization so narrow that we lose sight of the learner. After all, without the learner where would we be?

The other day I remarked to my wife, "Remember a few years ago when the waiter at the restaurant not only took your order but felt responsible for making sure that the right order got to your plate?"

Wouldn't it be terrible if people started making similar remarks about us educators. "Remember a few years ago when the educator not only understood my learning needs but worked hard to help me respond to them and then helped me to evaluate what additional learning might be needed?"

44. A Package From Barry

Can a present be like teaching?

Barry left for New Zealand this week. He and Joan sold the house, had some garage sales, picked out what they thought they'd need for living "down under" and put the rest in storage. I'm sure it was a chaotic scene. These types of moves always are.

Barry retired from teaching about 3 years ago. He had concluded a rewarding professional life as a university professor and it was now time to move on to other challenges. I remember the day he had described to me how he was getting tired of seeing the same things coming around again and again for the third and fourth time. His newer colleagues were charged with excitement about issues and problems that Barry had participated in "solving" years earlier. Clearly it was time for the "next generation" to take over the chase for elusive answers that no longer tempted Barry's interest.

Now you must understand that Barry is far from the typical image of a retired college professor. Sure, he still appears at his old office once in awhile and I have an idea he still enjoys wearing his tweed jackets with the patches on the sleeves. But that is where the retired college professor image ends. No, there is no way I could ever describe Barry as "typical."

Barry can probably best be described as mischievous! He delights in not only telling wonderful stories and jokes but also in setting great situations for practical jokes. At a conference Barry is usually right in the middle of any excitement that's going on. If a meeting hits a low spot Barry can always be depended upon to bring a sense of levity (sometimes absurdity) to shake everyone back into a more meaningful level of interaction. Barry is artful in using his humor to cut to key issues and concerns without creating a sense of threat.

I'm going to miss Barry!

Barry had mentioned in his farewell phone conversation with me that he had spent time looking for a special memento to send to me that would recognize our years of friendship. Last week a package arrived from Barry. It was a rather auspicious occasion. The package wasn't very large - it was one of those bubble insulated envelopes that we use for sending so many different things.

As I began to open the envelope I was challenged to think of what might be inside. How could you ever begin to select something to send to a friend that could capture the many interactions that we had together over the years? Certainly expense would not be an issue. In fact, one of the very enjoyable aspects of being with Barry was that there was never a scene at a restaurant over how to divide the bill. Barry was usually the one to quickly grab the check and pay for it. You could almost hear him saying that a restaurant bill was a very small price to pay for friendship. And then, of course, he would quickly segue into, "Did I ever tell you the joke about..."

Barry isn't much with letter writing. If you ever saw his handwriting you would understand. He much prefers the telephone and he is artful at calling when you would least expect him. Computers? Barry prides himself in not knowing where the on-off switch is and he has learned just enough high tech words (gigabyte, modem-shmodem, cyberspace) to make fun of all of the rest of us.

I tried bending the padded envelope and it seemed to bend quite easily. There wasn't anything very rigid inside. Which reminded me of how "unrigid" Barry is. In fact Barry makes a practice of not being rigid. For every rule or structure that you might want to create Barry is always there presenting a more flexible and much less rigid approach to the problem. "Why do we need a rule? Why don't we just try something and see how it works!" That is Barry.

What on earth could be in this envelope? The whole thought of trying to identify something special to send to a friend that would exemplify a relationship is mind boggling. What would I ever select to send to someone if I were leaving the country? How do I want someone to remember me? Sure I'm an educator. So, do I send a piece of chalk? Or better yet, how about a handful of overhead projector transparencies?

Would I send something that represents me or would I try to find something that represents our relationship? Would I be limited to only sending one thing or could I send a bunch of things? Maybe I could send a bunch of things but space them out over a long period of time so that as I thought of something else I could package it up and send it. What if I sent something and the other person didn't understand the link between the present and me?

Aha - that's an idea. Send something without an obvious reason. I could send something that got the other person thinking!! That would probably be the best idea. As an educator I'm always concerned with challenging the learner to think new ideas and to move beyond the obvious. That was it! That's how I'd do it. I'd send something to the other person that they wouldn't suspect and then they'd be challenged to try and figure out the inner meaning of what I'd sent. It's just like being an educator. Send an idea to a learner and then challenge the learner to understand and draw meaning from the idea.

One last piece of tape. The envelope is now open. What's this? Two old ties from Barry's closet. I wonder why he sent them.

45. Recycling The Future

Trying to draw meaning and
insight from the not-so-obvious

This morning's trip to the university got off to a somewhat auspicious start. I found myself stuck behind a rather large garbage truck with no room to pass. So I settled in for a slow ride.

Within a few seconds my attention was drawn to a large sign that had been affixed to the back of the truck. It was obviously part of a promotional campaign that the garbage collection company had created. They had decided upon a slogan that reflected today's concern for recycling and would create a positive image for the company.

The sign consisted of a large circle with three words arranged around the perimeter of the circle:

Recycling The Future

My mind still was not fully functioning at this early hour. I continued to drive behind the truck and stare at "Recycling The Future." I was in that "almost awake" stage when you can fool people into thinking that you are fully functioning but you really aren't.

After a few minutes the words slowly changed from being just a set of visual images to having meaning. I began to think about the meaning of the message that was being communicated.

Recycling The Future

What a great message! Or, was it? What do they mean with this message?

157

How can you recycle something like the future that has not yet existed. Maybe they should have stated their slogan as "Recycling The Past." That would have made a lot more sense. Recycling the past would be another way of saying that we must learn from our experiences and then make changes in the way we operate today - based upon our past and our reflections. The present gains so much more potential when we are able to learn from our past. "Recycling The Past" would have made so much more sense for this garbage truck.

But the sign didn't suggest I should recycle the past. No, it very clearly was urging me to get involved with "Recycling The Future."

What could they possibly mean by this absurd phrase? Maybe they were attempting to rewrite that old Yogi Berra phrase - "This is like *deja vu* all over again." At first the phrase seems to make sense but then you realize it really doesn't. (You probably remember some of the other famous Yogi Berra statements like, "Nobody goes there anymore; it's too crowded," "You can observe a lot just by watchin'," or "Baseball is 90% mental, the other half is physical".)

No, I don't think the garbage company was trying to be like Yogi Berra. So what were they trying to do?

Aha! Maybe it was a challenge for us to begin to think into the future, to see the problems, mistakes and errors that are sure to be made, and then to do something about it before we make all of those mistakes. That must be it. Now the message is beginning to make some sense. We have to be more forward thinking and learn to avoid mistakes before we actually make the mistakes. If we can learn to recycle before we even cycle for the first time we could become really powerful. What if today's youth became adept at Recycling The Future? Imagine what the future could bring. That's a tremendous concept. Whoever sold the garbage company on putting this slogan on their trucks should be congratulated. Maybe I should take some time and write a letter to the garbage company congratulating them on their insight. I wish more companies would do what they have done and challenge us to think beyond the obvious.

The truck began to signal a right turn. It's turning into that subdivision. And sure enough, it has the same recycle slogan written on the side of the truck. However, this time the words are not presented around the edges of a circle. No, this time the words appear in a straight line.

"Recycling: The Future"

Wait a minute, where did the colon come from? There was no colon on the back of the truck. Oops - I guess that changes the meaning. Maybe I won't write that congratulatory letter.

46. Teaching In Reverse

Trying to create a new frame of mind
to help with the challenge of evaluation.

Evaluation continues to be an area of high stress for most educators. It is clearly an area of concern but we often are not sure of how to go about it in a way that is meaningful to us and at the same time not costly in the time and energy that it takes. If we could only come up with a simple evaluative approach that is easy to do, can be implemented in a minute (without a lot of pre-planning), doesn't detract from our other activities, and clearly shows how we could improve the teaching/learning environment I'm sure we would use evaluation much, much more.

Sure, that opening paragraph sounds wonderful - sort of a "motherhood and apple pie" approach. Who can challenge such a logical view? The key is - how can we make it happen? How can we as educators move to a point where evaluation becomes second nature and a normal and accepted part of our responsibility?

As I have considered this question I have come to a point where it has become clear that mere evaluative techniques aren't going to be the answer. No, it's not going to be as simple as just finding the right instrument or approach that can be implemented. If it was that simple we would probably have a pocketful of those things and would be happily on our way to becoming a world class educational evaluator!

So, if it isn't techniques what is it? I think the answer lies more with our attitude and how we conceptualize the task of evaluation. In fact, I guess I feel that if we could adjust our understanding of exactly what evaluation is/could be we might be a lot further along the path of making effective use of evaluation in our work.

The first step, and probably the largest step, to being an evaluating educator is to have the right frame of mind. I could probably be pushed further to say that once we have the right frame of mind everything else will probably fall into place quite nicely. In fact, the identification of appropriate evaluation techniques and instruments will become a very minor task in the overall picture of things.

Now the next question - how do we go about identifying the "right" frame of mind? Well, sit down, I think I have the beginning of an answer. And, it isn't very complicated. It came to me yesterday as I was listening to a commentary on public radio. The commentator was talking about country and western music and how most songs follow a very familiar pattern. I'm sure you have heard the comment. It goes like this:

> "If you were to play a country and western song backwards the fellow who is the focus for the song would end up getting his dog back, his girlfriend back, and finally - he would get his pickup truck back."

It's a cute statement and a rather overworked commentary on country and western music.

But think about it for a minute. The idea of playing a record backward is intriguing! The differences which seem so subtle as we go from beginning to end suddenly become very apparent when we go from the end to the beginning. By reversing the view we see so much more. And, this simple switch in how I look at the lyrics of country and western music has me immediately evaluating that type of music and making a judgment or two based upon my own experiences in listening to country and western. And, of course, you really don't get to hear the song backwards - it's just a frame of mind.

That sounds like evaluation to me and no one forced me to do it! It was just a state of mind and a new way of looking at something that has been there all along. And, in the best of evaluative theory, it now presents me with the clear opportunity to do something about it, to make some informed judgments, based upon my evaluation. If I was a song writer I could decide whether to follow the "standard" scheme for my next song or try a variant.

What if we could play backwards the last teaching situation we were involved with? The idea is intriguing and very doable. Close your eyes and think about your learners leaving the room at the conclusion of your teaching. Then, slowly start rewinding your image to look at each point along the way - from ending to beginning. Most interesting!

Here are a few possible scenarios that might occur as you play the scene backwards:

> Ooops, there are no major shifts - no major points along the way! When I rewind the scene to the beginning it looks just like it did at the end! *(Did I really accomplish anything with my teaching?)*

> Wow, lots of major jumps and shifts as I move backwards. The beginning turns out to be a lot different than the end. *(Many changes occurred during my teaching. Though, was I involved with each of the shifts or was it a function of other things?)*

> Yes, there was a major shift. But who would have suspected we could have ended up at that point! *(Can I help make that shift occur again in the future?)*

> If I look really close I can see some very small and subtle shifts. *(Maybe I can fine tune things a bit to make the shift greater.)*

I have an idea that you are getting the picture. I'm not suggesting you implement any fancy form of an evaluation technique. No, just change your viewing of what you have done in your teaching. By slowly rewinding the scene to the beginning you will be able to compare the ending with the beginning and consider the path that was taken. Then you will be in a wonderful position to make any needed changes. I think that is what evaluation in education is all about.